DEEPER
PLACES

DEEPER
PLACES

Experiencing God in the Psalms

MATTHEW JACOBY

BakerBooks
a division of Baker Publishing Group
Grand Rapids, Michigan

Published by Baker Books
a division of Baker Publishing Group
P.O. Box 6287, Grand Rapids, MI 49516-6287
www.bakerbooks.com

Printed in the United States of America

Library of Congress Cataloging-in-Publication Data
Jacoby, Matthew, 1971–
        Deeper places : experiencing God in the Psalms / Matthew Jacoby.
        pages cm
        ISBN 978-0-8010-1520-5 (pbk.)
        1. Bible. O.T. Psalms—Devotional use. I. Title.
BS1430.54.J33 2013
223′.206—dc23   2012045922

13 14 15 16 17 18 19   7 6 5 4 3 2 1

CONTENTS

Download *two FREE* songs
from the world-acclaimed
Sons of Korah.

Visit **www.mytune.co** <http://www.mytune.co> and when prompted, enter in the **Promo Code** field the last 5 characters of the ISBN on the back of this book (no dashes).

Then enter your name, city, state, and country along with your email address. You will then be emailed a secure link to download your *FREE MP4* files from Sons of Korah.

INTRODUCTION

How lovely is your dwelling place,
  O LORD Almighty!
My soul yearns, even faints,
  for the courts of the LORD;
my heart and my flesh cry out
  for the living God.

                    Psalm 84:1–2

In Search of Reality

"I feel nothing." That is how many Christians would honestly respond when asked how they really feel about God. Beyond brief moments of inspiration and a basic underlying conviction, most people struggle to attain anything more than a remote and abstract idea about God. It is a symptom of a faith focused on concepts and propositions rather than real, personal encounter. We are children of our scientific culture, a culture obsessed with information about things. So we find our minds crammed with ideas about God, with concepts and facts about who God is and what he has done, but too often the reality of God is as remote to us as the reality of black holes and supernovas. It is little wonder, then, that we have no emotional connection with these facts. They are as abstract as a mathematical equation. It is true that three plus two equals five, but I cannot summon up any passion for that truth. I cannot love an idea. I can only love a person with whom I have some experience.

The Bible tells us that we can have a real relationship with the real God. In fact, this is commonly and correctly upheld by theologians to be the main purpose of human life: to know God, to glorify God, to enjoy God. The Good News is that no matter what we have or haven't done, we have access to God through Jesus Christ, who paid for all our sins. If we put our faith in him, we can become God's children.

If you have been a Christian for some time, you no doubt have heard this Good News again and again from hundreds of different angles. You probably have also been encouraged to *delight* in this message, to share it with others as the most wonderful news in the world, and even to rejoice in this message by singing songs of praise and thanks to God for what he has done. But what do you feel? Do you feel anything?

It may well be that the more you hear this message the more aggravatingly boring it becomes precisely because the only thing you feel when you hear it is the pressure to feel something you just don't feel. It can be like people continually telling you about a wonderful place but not telling you how to get there, or whether it is even possible to get there. As long as the Good News remains a matter of abstract facts, it will have little more effect on your life than your insurance policy has on the way you drive.

Great Expectations

I get the impression sometimes that a relationship with God, for many Christians, means little more than the possession of a spiritual status that gives them assurance of going to heaven when they die. In this case, being adopted as a child of God is more about knowing where one stands with God than actually knowing God himself in the relational sense. The whole thing is abstract and removed, as though the object of faith is a great contract in heaven rather than a person. Perhaps Christians tend to think like this because they have accommodated their expectations to their lack of real, personal experience. They have tried to normalize their failure to engage with God.

If we believe that Jesus has given us access to God, to be children of God and to love and be loved by God, then the clear implication is that we should *not* be content with knowing *about* God. We should not be content with anything less than knowing God with greater intimacy and more experiential engagement than we know and experience with any other person. Is such a thing possible? I imagine there is probably little within you that feels this to be in reach. You have probably accommodated your expectations to what you lack. It is difficult to live with a conviction *about* God while lacking any sense of real engagement *with* God. It is difficult to live in continual spiritual frustration, so we tend to lower our expectations and then try to justify those lowered expectations.

We will find lots of literature to help us justify our lowered expectations of God, but we won't find any in the Bible. The more we read the Bible, the harder we will have to work to maintain low expectations of God. For example, if Moses could speak with God "face to face, as a man speaks with his friend" (Exod. 33:11), how can we possibly justify an expectation of a lesser experience for us now? Is God's plan regressive? Are we to believe that what we have now is less than what Moses had? The more we read the Bible, the more frustrated we will get by the gaping incongruity between what is promised to us and what we actually have. This will bring us to a crucial junction of decision, and it is here that many people take the wrong turn.

Many people make the mistake of assuming that this tension between promise and reality is something to be avoided, that they must either lower their expectations of God or convince themselves that they have something they clearly don't have. But this very tension is a crucial element in the formation of a spiritual capacity to know God. I will say more about this in the following chapters, but suffice it to say now that the common avoidance of the tension between human reality and divine promise is evidence that we may have adopted inadequate notions of the spiritual life, to say the least. If we feel compelled to lower our expectations or embrace delusions in response to this tension, it is only because the expectations we had in the first place were seriously contaminated. It is not that we can ever have too high expectations of God. The contamination of our expectations is our misunderstanding of the *process* by which we attain what the Bible promises. It is not so much *what* we expect that is the initial problem but *how* we expect to get there. The failure of bad processes so often leads to disillusionment, which in turn leads to severely stunted expectations.

Beyond Token Piety

Read the Bible and pray. That is the nutshell prescription I was given as a young Christian for building my personal relationship with God. It is simple and achievable. You read God's Word, and you pray for yourself and others. That advice will get us started, but it won't be long before we realize that the spiritual journey, the experience of relating to God, is far from simple.

Due to the complexities of our dysfunctional hearts, we all begin our journey with God in the middle of a vast spiritual labyrinth. There is a sense of simplicity to be gained in the spiritual life, but it is not where we begin. If we make the spiritual life a simple matter of achieving goals using step-by-step processes and daily habits, it becomes more about personal achievement than real relationship. It is so easy, then, for the spiritual life to become little more than a religion of token gestures of piety that only serve to make us feel we have fulfilled our duty toward God. We should indeed read our Bibles and pray, but this advice is just too simplistic to be helpful to anyone who really wants to have a deep relationship with God.

So where do we look for an account of spirituality that is deeply relational, that is congruent with the complexities of life, that affirms the tensions of human existence, and that goes beyond simplistic and pragmatic notions of the spiritual life? To me, the answer is obvious, but not because of any brilliance on my part. It was an accidental discovery and by no means unique. The answer has always been right in front of our eyes and most probably on the tips of our tongues, if we have been a Christian for any length of time. It is contained in the book of the Bible that has been the most utilized part of Scripture (though less so in our time), the one most widely quoted (even in the Bible itself), and the one that successive generations of Bible scholars have acknowledged to be the defining example of biblical spirituality. I discovered it not initially because I was a Bible teacher but because I was a musician. I discovered a book of songs in the middle of my Bible.

The biblical Psalter, the book of Psalms, attracted me as a creative challenge long before I really came to understand it. It took years to understand the psalms, partly because the spirituality they portrayed is so countercultural to the spiritual environment I came into as a young Christian. With my band, Sons of Korah, I have worked for over fifteen years adapting the psalms to music and touring the world, singing them night after night. As time has gone on, I have found them doing unexpected things to me, and as a result, I have begun to understand what the purpose of this book actually is and how it can perform its function in my life.

The Trodden Path

It is always important, when interpreting a text of any type, to ask not only what it is *saying* but also what it was intended to *do*. What was its function? When we discover this, particularly with respect to the Bible, we discover the *meaning* of a text. The meaning of any part of Scripture is found when we discover what God is *doing* by having the text say what it is saying.

The Psalter is the most practical book of the Bible. It was not compiled just as a book to be read but as a tool to be used. For most of its history—since its final compilation somewhere after 500 BC—the contents of the book were not read by people or even read *to* people. Rather, the psalms were sung and prayed. This, I believe, is how the psalms yield their meaning. As I have discovered after many years of singing the psalms, it is by *using* the psalms that we begin to discover what they were actually intended to *do*.

The psalms show us what authentic spirituality looks like, and in this sense, they should shape our expectations of the spiritual life. The ultimate purpose of the psalms is not just to portray authentic spirituality but to draw us into the experience of those who went before us, those whose lives were used by God to create key spiritual precedents for us to base our lives upon. The psalms belong to a corporate spiritual context in which the acts of God in the lives of people were celebrated and commemorated annually. Many psalms were either written for or preserved specifically for commemoration festivals such as the Passover, the Feast of Weeks, and the Feast of Firstfruits. In these festivals, the people sought to find God in the present by connecting with his actions in the past. The psalms were seen as something akin to tracks in the jungle cut by those who had gone before. We are not left to work out the way for ourselves. The path has been trodden down, and we are invited to walk in this path and continue where the psalm writers left off.

David and the other writers of the psalms were the pioneers of the Spirit-filled life. The Spirit of God worked in and through them to show us what we can all discover for ourselves now that the Spirit of God has been poured out into our hearts. The psalms were written not to dictate religious habits or to achieve certain ends. They are expressions of the heart written to cultivate in us the very heart that they themselves express. They are given to us to shape our innermost desires and thereby to open up our capacity to live in relationship with God.

The fact that the psalms were written as songs should serve to underline the nature of their purpose. Music is the language of the heart, and it was for this language that the psalms were written. They were written not just to tell us *about* God but to draw us into an encounter *with* God. In this sense, the psalms both exemplify and potentially impart the very thing that the rest of the Bible directs us toward as the ultimate goal of human existence: a love relationship with God in which we glorify and enjoy God forever.

The biblical faith is not a religion we observe in order to achieve some level of status in God's favor. Faith is a relationship to be enjoyed and cherished. It is a matter of the heart, not to the exclusion of the intellect but flowing from the heart of love to the whole being and life of the individual. And faith is not individualistic. It has as its ultimate goal the reinvigoration of true community, the full expression of the kingdom of heaven on earth. Each of the psalms was selected and incorporated into Scripture by God's providence because it exemplified the ideals and goals of the biblical faith. The psalms became the primary tool by which the ancient faith of Abraham, Moses, and David was to be passed on from generation to generation.

Earthly Spirituality

If there was ever a time to search the Bible for a portrait of authentic spirituality, it is today. Our overentertained modern minds are prone to adopt highly romanticized notions of spirituality that inevitably lead us to disillusionment. A romanticized spirituality is one that creates a context in which we would like to live rather than the situation we actually have. We can tend to think that the expression of our hearts should be just like those of the worshipers in heaven. We can have a taste of heaven now, and, in fact, we are called to be the vessels through which the kingdom comes "on earth as it is in heaven." But, again, this is not a reality we begin with. We don't live in heaven; we live on earth. We live in an imperfect world, and we begin with highly dysfunctional spiritual capacities. Just because we can and should be experiencing certain heavenly realities does not mean that we are.

The wonderful thing about the psalms is that they show us how to begin where we are. We are not expected to begin with some heightened state of spiritual ecstasy. We can and must begin where we are. What we need is not a heavenly spirituality but an earthly spirituality that captures the present tension between what we have already and what remains unfulfilled. This is precisely what we have in the psalms.

The Purpose of This Book

To get in touch with the reality of God, we must first get in touch with the reality of our own situation. Self-realization is the first step toward any realization of the truth of things outside us. We cannot experience the reality of God while we remain in our fantasy-world cocoons.

The spiritual journey portrayed in the psalms, therefore, begins with the saddest and harshest realities of life. From here, the path winds upward into the embrace of God, and we find here a state of heart that, according to the psalms, is the ultimate state of happiness. From this happiness flows a joy that is both profound and indomitable. This is the shape of the journey we will take in this book. We will begin with a downhill descent into the valley of reality before ascending to the mountain of joy. On the way, we will visit the dominant experiences portrayed in the Psalter.

My purpose here is not to examine the Psalter itself as a piece of ancient literature. That is a valuable endeavor, and many books have been written about the psalms on that level. My intention here is to use the psalms as windows into the experiences of people—experiences that exemplify the life of faith from an inside perspective. The psalms are the expressions of people who had real interactions with a real God, and at their highest points, the psalms testify to an unshakable joy that must be desired by every person. But how did they get there? What does that road look like? These are questions that the psalms answer, and, in fact, I would even suggest that when we begin to use the psalms as a guide for this journey, we are beginning to grasp the meaning of this amazing biblical book of songs.

1

THE RICHNESS OF COMPLEXITY

You have made known to me the path of life;
you will fill me with joy in your presence,
with eternal pleasures at your right hand.

Psalm 16:11

The Complexity of Relationship

Relationships are complex. The more personal and intimate a relationship, the more complex it becomes. On the other hand, the less personal a relationship is, the simpler it becomes. The relationship between an employer and an employee is simple because it is definable in terms of an objectively formulated performance criteria. It is desirable in the workplace to keep relationships "professional" to avoid the complexities of the personal dimension. Simple equals efficient. The last thing you want in the workplace is to get bogged down in personal complexities.

We sometimes say that a couple has a "complex relationship" if we observe certain peculiarities in the way they relate to each other. And it is true that our emotional and spiritual dysfunction adds another layer of complexity to a relationship that compounds as the relationship deepens. However, quite apart from this consideration, complexity is the very essence of personal relationships. In personal relationships, people develop soul ties in the deepest part of the human spirit, and thus the relational connection becomes as mysterious as the human spirit itself.

To many people, the complexity of personal relationships is annoying, exasperating, and tiresome, and often these relationships are abandoned in a desire to return to a simpler form of relating. From this perspective, relationships are a kind of bog that obstructs the way forward.

The most fundamental implication of the twofold "love commandment" Jesus identifies as the summation of all God's commands (Mark 12:28–31) is this: Relationships are to be valued and enjoyed above everything else in life—first our relationship with God and then our relationships with others. Relationships, in other words, are to be treated as the highest of all ends. If we truly value relationships above everything else, then complexity will no longer be an annoyance. On the contrary, we will experience complexity as *richness*, something we delight in. When the highest desire we have is to enjoy a relationship as an end in itself, the mysterious complexity of the relationship creates more room for us to express and enjoy the relational experience.

The Nature of Relationship

Biblical faith is not a religion to observe or a code of ethics to follow. It is not even primarily a task to fulfill. Biblical faith is a *relationship to enjoy*. It is as simple as that. And yet, because it is a relationship, it is complex in the sense described above. The idea is simple: God wants to have a relationship with us. The experience, however, is complex, and it is this complexity that gives the experience its inexhaustible richness.

If we regard our relationship with God as a means to some other end, then, of course, as I have said, the complexity of the relationship will be an annoyance, and we will find ourselves trying to reduce the relationship to a simpler pragmatic form. We will want to simplify it down to *doing* certain things. We will want to feel we have fulfilled our spiritual duty by spending half an hour reading the Bible and praying each day and by serving in the church. We will begin to regard these spiritual exercises as we regard physical exercise.

Every second day I go for a run for about an hour. Afterward, I feel a sense of achievement. I feel satisfied that I am keeping myself fit, and I feel really good physically. I have made the mistake of treating my "spiritual health" in the same way. The idea of spiritual health is not particularly helpful because it makes it sound as though we can make ourselves spiritually healthy by doing certain things and bypassing relationship. But spiritual health cannot be divorced from healthy relationships—most crucially, a healthy relationship with God. The question is not "Are you spiritually healthy?" but "Do you have a healthy relationship with God and healthy relationships with other people?"

We cannot create a healthy relationship just by doing the right things. A relationship is not a task or an exercise. Relationship is a mode of life in which we choose to open ourselves to another person to be known and to know. It is therefore also a choice to become vulnerable to another person and to become, in a sense, dependent upon that person.

Imagine a woman says to her husband, "I just don't feel like you love me," to which the husband replies, "Well, just tell me what you want me to do!" I realize this is a common conversation between couples, which is why I use this example. The man, in this case, has completely missed the point, and, in fact, his reply would only compound his wife's concern. The woman wants a relationship with her husband and feels that their personal connection is waning. The man just wants to keep his wife happy so that he can get on with things that have become more important to him than the relationship itself. Hence, his wife's concerns are valid.

Implicitly, our response to God can be much like the response of the man in this example. We feel compelled to respond to the reality of God as we sense the weight of his claim upon us, but we tend to want a quick pragmatic answer to the situation. It is as though we are saying to God, "Just tell me what to do!" We tend to want our relationship with God to be as simple and pragmatic as that between an employer and an employee. We want a simple criteria by which we can feel satisfied that we have fulfilled our duties and kept God happy. This is how we get *religion*. Religion is our intuitive response to God's absolute claim upon us. It is what comes naturally, but it misses the point. God wants to have a relationship with us; he doesn't just want us to try to make him happy.

Two people trying to manipulate each other's emotions is not a relationship. It is not a surprise, however, if we think it is because we humans are constantly trying to create relationships with other people by impressing them, attracting them, and appealing to their desire to be "made happy." It is all highly dysfunctional and delusional. We sense the need for relationships, but in classic human fashion, we try to *make things happen* rather than seek to cultivate genuine, personal connections. It is no wonder, then, that we apply our dysfunctional interpersonal habits to God.

Healthy Relationship

So what does a healthy relationship with God look like? How does it express itself? The Sunday school response would be that it expresses itself in *obedience*. Obedience is the *fruit* of a healthy relationship with God. On the other hand, *disobedience* is a sign that there is something wrong with our relationship with God. The solution to disobedience, therefore, is not simply to start "doing the right things." If the fruit is bad, we don't focus on curing the fruit; we cure the tree. This is why so many Christians go around and around in circles when trying to deal with personal sin. They deal with it by trying harder not to sin. It never works. Something has to change in the heart. Inevitably, the problem comes down to some kind of *relational breakdown*, often between themselves and others, and always between themselves and God.

In one sense, our relationship with God is never entirely what it should be, as indeed is the case with all our relationships. For all our good intentions, we enter our relationships with a deeply corrupted nature. We are naturally selfish, defensive, and competitive. We inherited these inclinations from generations of our human ancestors who, following the first human beings, rejected God and tried to be gods unto themselves. This inherent spiritual dysfunction, as I said before, adds immeasurably to the complexity of relationships. We begin with a nature that is essentially disinclined toward good relationships. In light of this, it is not helpful to try to act out ideals. We can't enter a relationship as though we began from a state of complete spiritual flawlessness. When we begin a relationship, we bring with us a vast array of complex spiritual dysfunctions.

It's amazing how idealistic young, engaged couples can be about their relationship, and the same is true of young Christians. In the midst of their joy over the newly kindled relationship, these young romantics find it difficult to believe that everything isn't perfect. Deep down they know there are issues, but they are afraid of breaking the romantic facade by voicing the issues. *Conflict* therefore becomes the necessary growth pain.

I have spent a lot of time with young couples in premarital counseling, trying to prepare them for conflict without dampening their romantic joy. They hate hearing that conflict is inevitable, and they find it even harder to understand that constructive conflict is part of having a healthy relationship. This would not be the case if everything was ideal, but everything isn't ideal. So we need to conceive of healthy relationships in a way that takes our unfortunate personal/spiritual issues into consideration.

In this context, a healthy relationship is not a relationship without conflict; it is a relationship in which conflict is dealt with honestly and constructively. In a way, as strange as it sounds, we have to put right and wrong aside for this to happen. We know things are wrong; that's a given. The question is how to make things right, and we can't do this by pretending that things are right already. Often in premarital counseling, when I ask one person how he or she feels about the way the other person acts in this or that situation, the response is about how the person thinks he or she *should* feel, not how he or she really *does* feel. The intention is good, and they both want to honor their partner, but in a healthy relationship, we have to be able to express our feelings truthfully and constructively. For this reason, I spend a great deal of time teaching couples how to communicate. A lack of good communication is one of the key things that leads to unhealthy relationships.

Let's now apply these relational principles to our relationship with God. What does a healthy relationship with God look like? It looks like honest communication. It even looks like constructive conflict. We must take the idealistic boundaries out of our communication with God and allow for a range of expression that is congruent with the complexities of life. What does this look like? It looks like the psalms. Everything I have said so far is, I believe, necessary context for understanding the complexities of the psalms. There are many aspects of the psalms that people love and cherish, but many other aspects people find perplexing. This is because we come to the text with our ideals, and we analyze the psalms with questions such as, "Can you say that to God?" and "Are we allowed to pray that sort of thing?"

The psalmists were operating under completely different criteria. They were operating in the context of a relationship, and their expressions are *relational expressions*. Apart from the obviously didactic psalms, the psalmists weren't trying to give a theology lecture. They were just expressing how they felt, and that is not only valid but also a necessary part of a relationship. Psalm 74 is a good example of this. The psalmist makes a theologically outlandish statement: "Why have you rejected us forever, O God?" (v. 1). This is a little like my son crying out, "You don't love me anymore" when he is being disciplined. Of course, he knows this isn't true, but he wants to communicate his grief at having to sit alone in his room for a while. Apparently, God wants us to communicate as honestly and forthrightly as any child would with a parent. That is the disposition the psalms are implicitly inviting us to take before God.

The Complexity of the Psalms

If we understand the relational context of the Psalter, we are in a good position to understand the wide range of expressions within the psalms. The range of expression is indicative of the richness of the relationship. It is also congruent with the range of experiences we will inevitably have in life. To have a relationship with God is to share life with God. At the center of this sharing of life is a constant flow of communication: expressing joy when we are happy, showing gratitude when we are blessed, complaining when we feel let down, crying out when we feel abandoned, supplicating when we are in need, raging at injustice, delighting in goodness, lamenting hardship, and celebrating bounty.

The book of Psalms was not given to us to show us what angelic worship looks like. The psalms are an expression of what an authentic relationship looks like between human beings and God. They will therefore express all the complexities inherent in a relationship. From our perspective, they express the desire to feel loved, to be affirmed and validated, to feel secure, and so forth. This earthly spirituality, as I have called it, is also seen in the psalms in the ample expression they give to the complications of our human dysfunction. Human dysfunction does not guide these expressions, but our dysfunction does cause a constant tension in our relationship with God that must be brought to the surface with honest communication, as it must be in any relationship. This is what we see in the psalms.

God gave us the psalms for the same reason he gave us every other book of the Bible: to show us what he wants. The difference with the psalms is that, whereas other parts of the Bible may prescribe what God wants, the psalms *demonstrate* what God wants. He wants relationship. God wants to love and be loved. This is the summation of what the Bible tells us about God's will (Mark 12:28–31). As I said at the outset, relationships are complex, and the more personal they become, the more complex they become. We should embrace this complexity, which in turn means embracing honesty, which in turn means embracing diversity of expression.

Back to the Map

Popular Christian spirituality has tended to focus on just a few expressions, namely, the expressions that give voice to how we think we *should* feel. We tend to neglect expressing what we actually *do* feel. The ideal spiritual state is a state of devotion and joy, and so these become the dominant expressions in our spiritual vocabulary. These expressions are always appropriate in themselves. There will always be a part of us that can sincerely concur with these expressions, and we should indeed make these expressions our central theme. The problem here is not so much with what we do as with what we think we should *not* do. The issue expresses itself in our public worship, where it has become inconceivable that we would ever say something like, "O LORD God Almighty, how long will your anger smolder against the prayers of your people?" (Ps. 80:4).

I use this example from Psalm 80 because it is an overtly *communal* lament. All the psalms belonged in one way or another to the community expression, but some did so more explicitly, and this is the case with Psalm 80. The person who wrote this psalm was evidently so comfortable with expressing every kind of feeling to God that he was more than happy for these expressions to be made public and even to become a part of the public expression of the community. The words of Psalm 80 express how I often feel, but I cannot conceive of ever praying something like this out loud in a prayer meeting, let alone singing it in church as a congregational song. Is this a sign that we have moved from relationship into religion? Whatever the case, it is certainly a sign that we need to intentionally rethink how we understand Christian spirituality.

When it comes to rethinking the spiritual life, we may be inclined to look primarily and even exclusively to the New Testament writers. The psalms are clearly more directly poignant to the issue, but there is a tendency to view the psalms as outmoded expressions of an inferior type of relationship with God. This is an unfortunate view that prevents us from being informed by the psalms as we should. The difference between the Old and New Testament periods is not that the writers had a different sort of relationship with God. David, who wrote many of the psalms, was filled with the Spirit and understood himself to be a child of God by the grace of God alone. The difference between the Old and New Testament periods is that what was the experience of a privileged few (i.e., David and the prophets) under the old covenant is now available to *everyone* under the new covenant.

David's experience of a relationship with God, as expressed in his psalms, is therefore to be read as a kind of map for what this relationship can look like. We are given this map so that we can explore every part of the relational territory. Just as the Israelites were given the boundaries of the Promised Land so that they would know what they should take possession of, so we are given the psalms so we can know the extent of the relational experience we should possess. My concern is that we tend to settle for far less than what is actually given to us. We limit ourselves to a space so small that it is actually impossible for us to grow as God wants us to grow. If we are to grow in our relationship with God, we must revisit the map and move out into a full experience of the relationship with God that is portrayed for us there.

2

THE ART OF REORIENTATION

You have put me in the lowest pit,
  in the darkest depths.
Your wrath lies heavily upon me;
    you have overwhelmed me with all your waves.

                                        Psalm 88:6–7

Dissociation

Dissociation. It is not a commonly used term, but it's worth the vocabulary stretch because it takes us to the heart of the greatest challenge of the spiritual life. The terminology of dissociation is not used in the Bible, nor is it used in the theological systems that we are comfortable with. That is actually partly why I am using the word. What I will address in this chapter is certainly addressed throughout Scripture, but in different language and using different imagery. The message of the Bible is always in need of translation so that the force of its meaning might be felt through every linguistic obstacle that might present itself. One of the greatest obstacles between our hearts and the linguistic force of Scripture is familiarity. When words cease to have their designed effect, new words must be sought to instill timeless truth with fresh force. So it is that I am borrowing a term that belongs to the area of psychology in order to define a key role that I believe the Psalms can perform in our spiritual restoration.

Dissociation is why so many people get stuck in an abstract and detached experience of faith. As we begin our journey down the pathway that is cut for us in the book of Psalms, we come immediately to the great valley of reality that one must pass through in order to connect with truth. This is when dissociation kicks in. It behaves like the horse that skids to a halt before an obstacle that the rider intends to surmount. No matter how vehemently the rider chides and spurs on the horse, the horse remains obstinate in its refusal to progress beyond the perceived threat.

Dissociation is a defense mechanism in the human psyche that shields us from having to face the pain of certain traumas. We are all dissociative to some extent; we tolerate a "normal" dissociative level that remains unnoticed due to its being shared by all people. It is "just the way we are," and therefore we regard it as harmless because we tend to assess ourselves by our ability to interact with others in normal social situations. But when we assess ourselves by our ability to relate to God, we find a problem. This problem also emerges with irritating regularity as we seek to maintain long-term relationships that involve a high degree of vulnerability.

Dissociative identity disorder (sometimes inaccurately referred to as multiple personality disorder) is a psychological state that is most obviously manifest in people who have experienced extreme trauma, particularly in childhood. When a child experiences severe abuse, for example, in order to survive the inward barrage of guilt, self-hate, and rejection that would otherwise torment them, the mind may dissociate from that experience, creating a new identity that acts like a bandage for the pain. Dissociative identity disorder is a complex condition to address clinically because the therapist must try to find a way through many layers of identity to the real broken person underneath it all. The reason why it is necessary to get through all these defenses is so that the hurt child can face the reality of his or her pain. Until this happens, the individual is unable to engage with real life or genuinely connect with other people. He or she will constantly live through these other identities while the real person remains cocooned within a web of these identities. The connection between the real person and real life is severed.

The Pain of Reality

In order to connect with God, we have to emerge from our defensive cocoon and allow reality to dawn on us. We have to face the truth about ourselves and our human situation before we can embrace the truth of God. We cannot selectively embrace reality. Either we are willing to know the whole truth or we remain in delusion. The reality that every human being must face is inescapably painful because we have all experienced the deepest and most disfiguring trauma. Like a child torn from the arms of a parent, we have been rent from our natural soul tie to God. And this not by some external force, but rather, it is a propensity in ourselves that causes us to sabotage our most fundamental validating relationship. Our relationship to our adoring divine Father and our natural desire to live in his love is so much a part of our being that it is impossible for us to sabotage our relationship with God without inflicting great trauma on ourselves. Most Christians will readily accept this reality in a theoretical-theological sense, but few have allowed themselves to feel the personal trauma of this reality.

You cannot rejoice in salvation if you have not allowed yourself to feel the sadness of alienation.

It is impossible to live in such grievous tension with God without creating Band-Aid identities to enable oneself to detach sufficiently from the reality of the situation. Dissociation enables us to drown out the cries of the lonely orphaned child of God within us. We build our towers of self-validation, "making names for ourselves" (Gen. 11:4), projecting identities and competing with others to make these godlike identities believable. If the strength of believability is compromised, the pain of reality too easily wells up from underneath like volcanic lava. Ironically, when this happens, we are closer to reality, which is why Jesus declared that the "poor in spirit" are blessed (Matt. 5:3). It is they who are closest to truth. Their broken spirits give them greater exposure to reality.

Reconciliation with Reality

The spirituality of the Psalms begins with the pain of reconciliation. Christians rightly speak a great deal about the joy of reconciliation with God, but we tend to skip something. This omission is what accounts for the superficiality of our joy. Before the joy of reconciliation with God is the pain of reconciliation with reality. Our unwillingness to expose ourselves to the latter is what barricades us against the former.

The most dominant experience portrayed in the Psalms is that of people coming to terms with and exposing themselves to the full force of their harshest realities. In most cases this does not appear to be intentional on their part. It is an experience that they are drenched in as God sovereignly causes the harsh rain of real-world reality to fall upon them. But in other cases, we see the psalmists intentionally choosing to focus on and grieve over what they believe grieves the heart of God. It is a choice that they make to align their hearts with the heart of God.

It is possible to read the lament psalms and find only the negative expression of grief and pain. But what is in fact being expressed here, we should not miss, is the awakening of the heart. In one way or another the psalmist is being reconciled with reality. The lament psalms have been referred to as "psalms of disorientation," and this is descriptive of the experience that is being expressed in them. But often the experience the lamenting psalmists refer to is that of being stripped of things that gave them a false sense of orientation and security. In this way, the psalmists are enabled to feel what and who they really are. The lament psalms can therefore be thought of as psalms of *reorientation*. The tragedy of finding oneself in a mirage becomes the beginning of an about-face that puts the psalmist face to face with God. This is why we find some of the deepest expressions of joy in the Psalms coming from context of severe hardship.

The relationship between sorrow and joy in the Psalms is profound, and I will devote a lot of space to exploring this connection. This relationship is the key to understanding why our spirituality can seem so inescapably superficial at times and discovering how we can break through this to much deeper places in our relationship with God.

3

THE PURSUIT OF SADNESS

The LORD looks down from heaven
  on the sons of men
to see if there are any who understand,
  any who seek God.
All have turned aside,
  they have together become corrupt;
there is no one who does good,
  not even one.

Psalm 14:2–3

The Sadness of God

God is sad. This is the most urgent reality that faces us. God suffers a deep and inconsolable sadness. It may seem strange that such a thing could be said of the eternal, all-powerful God. The greatness of his being may suggest that he is invulnerable to suffering. But, in choosing to love, God indeed made himself vulnerable, because if love is unrequited, it becomes the source of immense grief.

How could God not be sad? If he loves human beings as his own children, how could he not be deeply grief stricken by the plight of humanity? How inconceivably terrible must the weight of the collective suffering of humanity be to God! I can barely cope with the thought that even one small child should be subject to physical and emotional torment, and yet God has to bear the weight of the suffering of billions of his children. If my love for my children is any indication of God's love for those he has created, then I cannot conceive how he can bear such grief.

More terrible still is the fact that this suffering is ultimately caused by human beings having severed the bond of love between themselves and God. It is terrible enough to have to look upon the suffering of those you love when you can do nothing about it. But it is worse still when you *can* do something about the situation that causes the suffering, but your offer of love and reconciliation is rejected. That God's children would rather suffer in alienation and destitution than be reconciled to God is surely the most tragic situation imaginable.

Sadness is the unfulfilled capacity for joy. God is in anguish over his children because they are his highest joy. The greater the joy, the greater the sorrow when the object of one's joy is lost. But the inverse is also true. The greater the sorrow over a lost child, the greater the joy when the child is found again. And so, as Jesus said, "There is rejoicing in the presence of the angels of God over one sinner who repents" (Luke 15:10). God's sadness flows from his joy, and the increase of his joy in being reconciled to his children flows from his sadness at having lost them. If sadness is unfulfilled joy, then joy is the fulfillment of sadness.

If it is true that God is deeply grieved, and according to the Bible it is, then the cause of this grief must of necessity become our primary concern. To embrace God is to allow his desires to rule in our hearts. To know God is to share his joy and therefore also his grief. If any person is to love God, he or she must be prepared to grieve over the things that grieve God. To come to God is to have our hearts broken by God's sadness, not only for the world he loves but also for us. To be embraced by God is to be shattered by the revelation of all that grieves God in our lives. It is to be devastated by the reality that *we* are the cause of the greatest suffering in the universe: the suffering of God.

Embracing the Sadness of God

We make God sad. There are things in our lives that grieve God: our propensity to stray from him, our defensiveness against his claim upon us, our disregard of his kindness, and our lack of trust in his love expressed in actions that blatantly disregard his directives to us. This, in every human being to a lesser or greater extent, is what causes the suffering of God. There is no greater love than that which God has for his children, so there is no greater sadness than when God's children spurn his love. We have all done it, we all do it, and you and I are probably doing it right now. Such is the propensity of human nature to autonomy and independence that even the most sanctified of hearts will not be free of this offense. To deny this is, according to the apostle John, to deceive ourselves (1 John 1:6).

The spirituality of the psalms begins with this self-realization. Specifically, it begins with the psalmist feeling the painful tension between his sense of primary kinship with God and his propensity to grieve the one who so persistently loves and blesses him. This is, to use a musical term, the root note in the psalms of alienation. The theological term for it is *penitence*. It is not that all the psalms of alienation explicitly begin with expressions of penitence, but rather penitence appears to be a primary aspect of the initial approach to God from the position of alienation.

I hesitate to use a traditional term, in this case *penitence*, because of its idealized acceptance in Christian piety. The experience portrayed in the penitential psalms is not the abstract acceptance of basic depravity that Christians acquiesce to for the sake of theological correctness. Nor is it the institutionalized woe-is-me routine of would-be zealous piety.

Penitence in the psalms is not a building block for a pious identity but rather something deeply relational. It is the emerging sense of a terrible relational rift between the individual and God. The experience is akin to that of a person with painful injuries who is feeling the results of the gradual abatement of the anesthetic that has kept the pain at bay. In the psalms, this is the result of the initial turn toward God that occurs when life has become bitter and calamitous. The fruit of the Spirit manifested in the psalmist's heart in these moments compels him to acknowledge the relational tragedy in the midst of whatever circumstantial dilemma he faces. This prevents him from the usual fist-shaking approach of those who blindly imagine God as an abstract source of insurance rather than a divine Father. The relational rift that provides the disturbance in the penitential psalms is that between the God who loves with such persistence and the object of his love, who spurns that love with equal persistence. Penitence occurs when God's persistence wins.

4

THE JOY OF BROKENNESS

> The sacrifices of God are a broken spirit;
> a broken and contrite heart,
> O God, you will not despise.
>
> Psalm 51:17

The Ocean and the Shell

God is everywhere. We are engulfed in his presence. His presence is like the water of a vast ocean in which we are deeply immersed and suspended. "You hem me in—behind and before," says the psalmist (Ps. 139:5), "Where can I go from your Spirit? Where can I flee from your presence?" (v. 7). God is everywhere, all around us, pressing in upon us as the ocean presses in upon a submerged object. How is it then that God can remain so seemingly distant and remote from us? How is it that we can feel so alienated from God if we are so engulfed in his presence?

The reason for this is because we have developed a thick shell, like the thick steel casing of a deep-sea submarine. The shell keeps the infinite ocean of God's presence from touching us. We can be in the ocean and yet remain largely unaffected by it. Inside our shell, the only sense we have of the ocean is the abstract idea that it is out there beyond our immediate perceptible reality. Inside our shell, it is possible, even common, for us to become so accustomed to and focused on our small, incarcerated lives that we forget and maybe even begin to doubt the existence of the ocean in which we are submerged.

Occasionally, however, we find ourselves submerged deeper into the ocean, perhaps through curiosity, perhaps just by accident. When this happens, we begin to feel a strange sensation as our shell groans under the pressure of the ocean. This sensation is often the first indication to us that there is something beyond the little world in which we live. But our immediate reaction, so deeply intuitive that it is often subconscious, is to move upward and away from where the pressure is exerted upon us. We do this because the groaning reminds us of the destructibility of our shell, and the prospect of our shell being broken is inconceivable to us. We cannot conceive of any other way of living. The ocean terrifies us because we have become accustomed to our incarceration inside the shell. But that is nevertheless what we are: *incarcerated*. We are trapped in our own defensiveness and self-deceit. We are trapped by our own desire to be autonomous and sovereign. This is, of course, another metaphoric expression of the biblical notion of hard-heartedness.

Equalization

We have become shell creatures, but we were not made this way. We built our shell because we wanted to become lord of our own universe, so we had to create a universe for ourselves over which it was possible to exert some control. The more control we desired, the smaller our universe became. And so we find ourselves in this thick shell, sealed off from the ocean of God's presence, which surrounds us. In this sense, we are also sealed off from reality. This creates a clash of states, as is the case with any submerged, sealed object such as a submarine.

It is only with great difficulty that we can submerge a sealed, air-filled object because the water pressure compels it to float upward and away from where the pressure is exerted.

What causes this is the disparity between the low density of the air inside the object and the high density of the water outside the object. The deeper the object goes, the greater the clash because of the higher water density at greater depths. Divers have to deal with this issue when they go deep into the ocean. The air pressure inside their ears is at odds with the water pressure outside their ears. To prevent this clash, and the pain it causes, they have to equalize. They do this by pinching their nose and blowing against their closed nose and mouth, forcing externally pressurized air into the ear through the nasal cavity. Equalization occurs when the inner state is brought into conformity with the outer state. With divers, this is possible only to a certain depth.

Deep-sea fish are able to live in the areas of the ocean where the pressure is the greatest because they have ways of keeping their internal pressure the same as that of the water around them. Many deep-sea fish do not have any excess body cavities, and their bodies are soft and flexible. The deep is their natural environment, and they are able to move about in it and remain suspended without the resistance of any disparity between inner and outer pressure.

We are, to continue with the metaphor, like deep-sea fish. If the presence of God is to be likened to an infinite ocean, then our natural environment—the environment that allows us to move most freely and uninhibited—is in the deepest connection with his presence. When we are in the deep ocean and the ocean fills us, a kind of equalization occurs. Our inner state is in conformity with the external reality of God, so there is no painful conflict between our internal state and the external reality. We are able to live in a state of rest, suspended weightlessly in complete conformity with God.

However, by developing a shell to shut out the reality of God and create a self-determined internal environment, we have created a disparity. We then live in an environment that stifles everything we were made to be. Life is cumbersome, and we live with a constant conflict between our internal state and external reality. And though we are constantly repelling ourselves away from the deep, we are unable to escape the conflict completely because God is indeed infinite and everywhere. And so the cry of the psalmist is poignant when he asks, "Where can I go from your Spirit? Where can I flee from your presence?" (Ps. 139:7). The answer can be the most wonderful truth or the most terrible. It depends on whether or not we are equalized.

Journey into the Deep

The first step in the spiritual journey portrayed in the psalms is the breaking of the shell that allows us to disassociate from reality. The psalms of lament are like the groaning and cracking of this shell. The pain of brokenness is the necessary pathway to the joy of freedom.

This process is fascinating and remarkably familiar to anyone who has made this journey. The cries of alienation lead the psalmist deeper into God. We can sense the tension in the cries, tension between the psalmist's experience and the reality of God. The psalmist feels forsaken, yet God is telling him that he is with him. He seeks God on the strength of the assurances of his Word, the truth of which, however, still remains abstract.

As he goes deeper, the tension increases until finally the shell starts to crack. It is similar to a submarine being submerged where the pressure is too great. The steel groans ominously. Then bolts start to blow out, and water begins to spray into the cabin. This is what happens when the lamenting psalmist is suddenly invigorated by a sense of God's reality. This is the moment when God's promises cease to be abstract and when faith is awakened by the cool, invigorating spray of his presence. The experience compels the psalmist to push deeper into God until finally the cracks in the shell are gaping and the water is gushing in.

When the shell is finally broken, a wonderful experience of happiness ensues. It is a happiness that is known only by those who have encountered God in this way. It feels like being suspended weightlessly in the ocean of God's presence. Even though we feel the immense pressure of his presence bearing down upon us, we still feel weightless because we are equalized. His presence fills us, allowing us to be suspended in that deep place without being propelled away from where the pressure is exerted.

The joy of the broken is the joy of those who are set free, like fish in the ocean, free to move and live in their natural environment without the cumbersome shell that shields them from reality. The principle underlying this spiritual journey of the Psalter is succinctly summed up in the words of Psalm 126: "Those who sow in tears will reap with songs of joy" (v. 5). It is a different metaphor, but not entirely. Only when a seed is submerged can it break open and the process of growth begin.

This principle, which is so abundantly demonstrated in the psalms, also lies behind the strange and otherwise absurd injunction of James: "Grieve, mourn and wail. Change your laughter to mourning and your joy to gloom" (James 4:9). It is not that James envisages the fruit of the Christian life to be sadness. On the contrary, the fruit of knowing God is *fullness of joy*. But to grow fruit you need a seed, and the seed of joy is sadness. As a Jew evidently steeped in the wisdom literature of the Old Testament, James understood that if we sow in sadness, we will reap the joy of salvation. He says, "Humble yourselves before the Lord, and he will lift you up" (4:10). Jesus makes the same point when he says, "Blessed are you who weep now, for you will laugh," and, "Woe to you who laugh now, for you will mourn and weep" (Luke 6:21, 25).

It is a terrible thing to fabricate joy when the sadness of God remains unconsoled, to dress the wound of offense that grieves God and to say, "Peace, peace, . . . when there is no peace" (Jer. 6:14). The love of God compels us to allow our shells to be crushed by the sadness of God. And as we sow in tears, as we allow our hearts to be broken open with the sadness of God, we will surely then know the joy of God as it floods in through the cracks of our brokenness.

5

OPTIMISTIC REALISM

Why do the nations conspire
and the peoples plot in vain?
The kings of the earth take their stand
and the rulers gather together
against the Lord
and against his Anointed One.

Psalm 2:1–2

The Context of Joy

The lament is the most dominant genre of expression in the Psalter, simply because it is where the writers of the psalms most often found themselves. The strong theme of lament in the Psalter does not mean that the ultimate purpose of the Psalter is to make people sad. On the contrary, the psalms are always oriented toward finding joy, and this joy is abundantly expressed in the book. The fact that the book of Psalms ends with a series of jubilant psalms demonstrates this direction. But we must recognize the context for that joy.

In the psalms, joy is always connected with salvation. The backdrop for the psalms is the same backdrop for the entire narrative of the Bible, and it is within this narrative that the psalms must be read. That backdrop is the universal human tragedy: the alienation of humans from God, the spread of evil, and the corruption of the natural world. If the psalms are sad, it is because they were written by people who were in touch with this reality. The pain of this reality, however, appears to be the very thing that amplified the joy of their salvation. The greater sensitivity we have toward a problem, the greater our joy in the solution. And so it is with every jubilant psalm. They are grounded in an acute awareness of the tragedy of the human situation.

Those of us who live in wealthy countries are obviously not immune to tragedy, but we are far less vulnerable than the majority of humanity. To some extent, we have been able to free ourselves from what the writer of Psalm 73 refers to as "the burdens common to man" (v. 5). But because of the benefits of our situation, we are dangerously prone to developing delusional aspirations of being in control. We have become so comfortable in our little self-created heavens that we are prone to forget what the majority of human beings have to put up with.

So when suffering does strike us, as it inevitably does at times in our lives, we have an extra burden to deal with on top of our grief—the burden of a kind of culture shock. We have to deal not just with loss or pain but also with the shock of being thrown into the deep end of a reality from which we had disassociated ourselves. It is one thing to suffer, but it is another to be shocked by suffering, to feel as though God left the window to our little heaven ajar, allowing the storms of a different reality to strike us. We are prone to react to personal misfortune with the cry, "Why me?" But when this question arises within us, we must hear the implied answer of the rest of humanity: "Why not you?" The question is not, "Why should I suffer?" but rather, "Why should I be exempt from the suffering that is common to all humankind?"

Outside the Garden

We don't live in the Garden of Eden anymore. We look forward to a new heavenly earth that is the restoration of Eden (Rev. 21–22), and even now that restoration process is working in the world through God's ever-present kingdom. But we still live outside the garden. The world is broken.

This fact lies at the center of the biblical worldview, and the spirituality of the psalms can be understood only from within this worldview.

The first three chapters of the book of Genesis graphically and succinctly portray the fall of humankind from a position of authority and goodness into alienation from God and moral/spiritual corruption. When Adam fell, the world over which he was made responsible fell with him into a state of corruption. In disconnecting himself from God, in desiring to be a god unto himself, he abdicated his position as prince of this world, effectively giving this position over to that fallen angel, Satan, who had so tempted him to rebel against God. As "prince of this world" (John 12:31; 14:30; 16:11), Satan was thus free to roam throughout the earth and sow evil in his path (Job 1:7; Matt. 13:25).

God is grieved over the choices of his children. Into their hands he placed the most wonderful gift imaginable, and they threw it to the ground in contempt. Their terrible offense against God poisoned the very air they would have to breathe. The ground they would walk on would from that moment spurn their presence, as one would regurgitate poisoned food. Creation would groan under the weight of such an offense (Rom. 8:20, 22), and the very crust and atmosphere of the planet would, as though it had a heart to be grieved, be constantly vying against its caretaker, who had so terribly betrayed it. Such is the curse that humans would have to suffer for their sin.

> Cursed is the ground because of you;
>   in pain you shall eat of it all the days of your life;
> thorns and thistles it shall bring forth for you;
>   and you shall eat the plants of the field.
> By the sweat of your face
>   you shall eat bread,

> till you return to the ground,
>> for out of it you were taken;
> for you are dust,
>> and to dust you shall return. (Gen. 3:17–19 ESV)

This is the world we live in still. The curse remains. If we entrust ourselves to Jesus Christ, he takes away the guilt of our sin but not the full consequence of the corporate sin of all humankind. That lies in the future, in the new heavens and the new earth (Rev. 21–22). In the meantime, the task of every Christian is to give the world a taste of the future in the present. We are called to minister healing and restoration in this broken world. The significance of our work is to herald the coming kingdom that is even now present in our lives and in our works.

The present work of God through his people is not designed to make people more content with living in the world as it is. On the contrary, the taste of heaven that we receive from God now is designed to make us *less content* with the world as it is. God wants us to increasingly live in anticipation of his coming transformation, which will culminate in the return of Christ and the final destruction of all evil. There is a sense in which the present works of God only serve to drive the sadness of God deeper into our being, for once you have been warmed by the presence of God, you will feel the coldness of this destitute world with much greater intensity.

An Empathetic Spirituality

Jesus did not promise his followers that they would be immune to suffering, and he did not expect that when they suffered they should not be grieved at their suffering. The experience of joy that Peter, Paul, and others had in the midst of their persecution was directly related to their sense of being counted worthy to be persecuted for Jesus's name (Acts 5:41). The fact that they experienced joy in this situation did not mean they did not feel the pain of the suffering. In the psalms, a profound joy is cultivated in the very place of suffering precisely because the psalmists allowed themselves to embrace the reality of their suffering. It broke them open to the fullness of reality and made it possible for them to encounter God.

Persecution aside, Jesus certainly envisioned his people being in the same boat as everyone else. The parable of the houses on the rock and the sand portrays the storms of life striking both houses with equal force. The promise of Jesus is that if his people abide by his words they will stand through the storms of life (Matt. 7:24–27). Jesus wants us in the same boat as everyone else because the boat is broken and he wants us to fix it.

We may not be suffering now like many in the world. Yet given the natural spiritual bond of kinship between all humankind, it is impossible to disassociate from the suffering of another person without becoming highly dysfunctional. Other people are part of our own personhood. We are defined in relationship, first with God and then with others. The Christian who says I no longer need to lament because I am saved has disassociated himself from the rest of the world that is still lost.

The spirituality of the psalms is not self-indulgent, but it is empathetic to the core. In many cases, the psalmists lament not over their own suffering but over that of others. In Psalm 80, for example, a Judean psalmist laments over the destruction of the northern tribes of Israel (722 BC). Throughout the history of the divided kingdom, a great rivalry existed between the northern kingdom of Israel and the southern kingdom of Judah, and yet when Israel was destroyed by the Assyrians, the people of Judah responded with a corporate lament that treated the tragedy of the Assyrian conquest of Israel as though it were their own tragedy:

> Your vine is cut down, it is burned with fire;
>> at your rebuke your people perish.
> Let your hand rest on the man at your right hand,
>> the son of man you have raised up for yourself.
> Then we will not turn away from you;
>> revive us, and we will call on your name.
>
> Restore us, O LORD God Almighty;
>> make your face shine upon us,
>> that we may be saved. (vv. 16–19)

This is empathetic grief, and it is an essential attribute of biblical spirituality.

It is strange that the practice of corporate lamentation has become so countercultural in the Christian church today. It is right that we should pursue joy, but we don't gain joy by shutting down the expression of grief. Moreover, how can we represent the one who suffered *for* the world if we are not willing to suffer grief in empathy *with* the world? The discarding of the genre of lament from our corporate worship repertoire is, I believe, the greatest omission in the worship practices of the church today. Besides the obvious lack of empathy that this omission expresses, it also causes us to be unprepared for the harsh realities of life when they come our way. The more empathetic we become, the more we acclimate our hearts to reality, saving ourselves from the culture shock of suffering. Grief will drive us to God. But if in our hearts we believe we are entitled to immunity from suffering, the culture shock that comes when tragedy strikes will almost certainly embitter us against God.

Permission to Suffer

The psalms portray a spirituality that is shaped to a large degree by suffering. For those who go through extreme times of bereavement, sickness, and heartache, this is what makes the psalms so pertinent. But for many people, the strong perspective of suffering in the psalms is what alienates them from these spiritual expressions.

The world that the writers of the psalms lived in was a world in which the pervasive corruption caused by the fall of humankind had much fuller expression than it has in our modern, Western environment. The people who wrote the psalms had no illusions about the nature of reality. They would no doubt have seen, and even suffered, the cruelties of ancient warfare. They would have suffered famine, plague, and the bereavement of those closest to them.

As I have said, we in the Western world have managed to curb the expression of this persistent reality to a large extent. It may even be possible for us to entertain delusions of invulnerability. To the extent that this is the case, however, we find ourselves alienated from the context within which the psalms make sense. As most of us know all too well, it doesn't take much for reality to crash in upon us, and it is often when this happens that the psalms begin to resonate with us again.

To understand the psalms, therefore, we have to embrace the context in which the psalms were written. For those who suffer, this imperative may seem to be inapplicable, since it would seem that, when we suffer, reality embraces us. But that is not necessarily the case. What we see in the many lament psalms is a process in which the individual or community is deliberately laying open the reality of their situation, or simply their feelings about their situation, as though it were opening up an infected wound. This is a vital process, and it is repeated in psalm after psalm.

> Save me, O God,
>   for the waters have come up to my neck.
> I sink in the miry depths,
>   where there is no foothold.
> I have come into the deep waters;
>   the floods engulf me. (Ps. 69:1–2)

> For my days vanish like smoke;
>   my bones burn like glowing embers.
> My heart is blighted and withered like grass;
>   I forget to eat my food.
> Because of my loud groaning
>   I am reduced to skin and bones.
> I am like a desert owl,
>   like an owl among the ruins.
> I lie awake; I have become
>   like a bird alone on a roof.
> All day long my enemies taunt me;
>   those who rail against me use my name as a curse.
> For I eat ashes as my food
>   and mingle my drink with tears. (Ps. 102:3–9)

These expressions of grief and pain, and the many others like them in the book of Psalms, are not a self-indulgent wallowing in misery. The full expression of grief is vital for moving out of grief. *Grief must be exhausted in order to be alleviated.*

The use of metaphor is common throughout the psalms and not least in the lament psalms, where it is a vital part of the catharsis of grieving. The lamenting psalmists use the imagery of drowning, of being surrounded by beasts, of being emptied like a jar, of melting like wax, and of burning like embers to describe how they feel. There is a healing effect in expression. The grief of the psalmists was expressed like this not primarily for the benefit of someone else but for the exhaustion of grief itself. And yet there is indeed great benefit for us all in these expressions.

The lament psalms provide an empathetic touchstone for those who suffer in the same way. They not only give us permission to grieve but also encourage us to express our grief fully before God. As we do this, we can begin to appropriate the compassion of the God who is no stranger to suffering. In this way, the psalms show us how to suffer. They call us to cry on God's shoulder and exhaust our grief in the presence of the most empathetic listener in the universe.

The Optimism of Sadness

The lament psalms demonstrate an optimistic realism. They demonstrate a sober acquaintance with the harshest realities of the world, and yet they are by no means pessimistic as a result of this acknowledgment. Pessimism is the attitude of hopelessness. It is the belief that nothing will get any better. If I am told by my doctor that I am overweight and in danger of heart disease, I would not call him a pessimist, and I would not be a pessimist for recognizing this fact. If I wallow in despair, believing that there is no way to change this situation, then I would be a pessimist. But if I, in response to my doctor's diagnosis, begin to change my diet and exercise, then I demonstrate that a reality check can do wonderful things to motivate us to seek a solution to our problem. An optimism that will not face reality is only delusion. But to face reality and nevertheless believe that there is a solution is the most powerful form of optimism. This is the optimism of faith that is expressed in the psalms.

The laments are not just expressions of grief; they are expressions of grief *before God*. This is the key. As we open our hearts to let out the pain, we thereby also open our hearts to receive consolation, and our consolation is God's preoccupation with restoration. In the psalms, the most celebrated aspect of God's activity in the world is his perpetual work of salvation. The God of the psalms is the great Redeemer of his people. He is gracious, merciful, and compassionate; he lifts up those who are bowed down; he answers those who are in distress; he comforts those in pain; he provides for those in need. If I were to quote here every expression of these truths in the psalms, I would end up copying most of the Psalter.

Behind the cries of the lament psalms lies a deeply ingrained optimism about God's willingness to act for the restoration of his people. These moments of pain are what most often bring this optimism to the surface. It is against the dark backdrop of seemingly hopeless circumstances that the luminous optimism of faith stands out with such clarity and can then be intentionally exercised. So it is that many of the most profound expressions of joy in the psalms arise in the midst of the most grievous circumstances. It is a remarkable feature of the psalms, and one I will discuss further as we move upward out of the genre of lament toward the mountaintop of biblical joy, which is the goal of the journey of the psalms.

6

THE ANATOMY
OF HAPPINESS

Blessed are those you choose
  and bring near to live in your courts!
We are filled with the good things of your house,
  of your holy temple.

Psalm 65:4

The Pursuit of Happiness

You want to be happy. Admit it; it's okay. I want the same thing. Everyone does. Your longing for happiness is valid. If I love someone, my love inevitably expresses itself in my desire for his or her happiness. I want my children to be happy, and as a child of God, I know that God wants me to be happy.

The very first psalm in the Psalter is essentially written to answer the question about how we can be truly happy. The placing of this psalm at the opening of the Psalter was intentional. It was put there to introduce what the editors of the Psalter saw as the message of the book they were compiling. They recognized that the Psalter as a whole shows us a pathway by which we can attain true happiness. It is a pathway that is described not in terms of outward actions but in terms of an inward journey of faith. The psalms show us the disposition of a godly person in every kind of life circumstance. Whether he be in hardship or prosperity, as Psalm 1 says, because he is walking in the ways of God, his leaves shall never wither.

> Blessed is the man
>   who does not walk in the counsel of the wicked
> or stand in the way of sinners
>   or sit in the seat of mockers.

> But his delight is in the law of the LORD,
>> and on his law he meditates day and night.
> He is like a tree planted by streams of water,
>> which yields its fruit in season
> and whose leaf does not wither.
>> Whatever he does prospers. (Ps. 1:1–3)

The Hebrew word translated here as "blessed" was used to describe what most modern English speakers call "happiness." It is used to describe the most desirable state of being possible for a human being. The word *happiness* seems to have become the most intuitive word in our usage of the English language to express a universal, if largely undefined, desire.

Many Christian teachers avoid using the word *happiness*, believing it has been diluted and even defiled by popular usage. I believe, however, that God speaks the language of the world he loves. He speaks to the heart, and therefore he wants to use our heart language. If I were to choose a word to describe the most desirable state of being portrayed in the psalms, I would choose the word *happiness*. Joy is the feeling that arises from being happy. The psalms describe the process of attaining joy as an experience flowing from happiness.

Defining Happiness

To what are people referring when they use the word *happiness* to express their deepest longing? What is happiness? The word itself is an indeterminate term that we use to refer to the most desirable state of being imaginable for us. Its meaning for each of us consists of fragments of positive experiences we have had, the memory of which makes us conscious of an indefinable absence of something fundamental to our being. This sense of absence creates a longing to revisit the experiences that we denote under the one broad heading of "happiness." What people most fail to do is to analyze what it was in these past experiences that made them feel good and why these experiences did not last.

We are inevitably drawn, it seems, to methods of becoming happy over which we can exercise some control. It is altogether counterintuitive to seek fulfillment in something we cannot control. We will never feel that we have fulfilled a desire if the fulfillment does not seem secure. To have something one might easily lose is, we sense, potentially worse than not having it at all. And so we seek fulfillment in things we can potentially control. We are naturally drawn, therefore, to things, places, and activities. If we felt validated and significant in a newly kindled romantic relationship, then we will seek a new romantic attachment. If we felt peaceful and content with a new home or with an improved financial status, we will strive to acquire a better home or gain a higher level of financial security. If we felt invigorated and purposeful in a certain activity, we will return to that activity. In all these things, we fail to understand the essential nature of our desires and their relationships to external circumstances.

If I were to summarize the central principle that God reveals to us in the psalms, it would be this: *rightly oriented desire*. This, as I shall demonstrate, is the key to happiness. Whereas the biblical narratives speak of actions, the psalms express desire. They also demonstrate the journey by which desire itself finds its ultimate fulfillment. This elusive thing we call happiness is beautifully and abundantly expressed in the psalms in a way that enables us to understand much about the anatomy and source of happiness. And so I will use the psalms to define what it is that you and I really long for.

The Origin of Happiness

You may think that the best place to begin to analyze the experience of happiness in the psalms is in the jubilant praise psalms. These moments of jubilation in the psalms are indeed expressions of happiness, but for the sake of clarity, they are not the best starting point. The experience of jubilation is an intermittent experience in the broad continuum of the spiritual life portrayed in the psalms.

I once visited Lake Michigan on a very windy day and noticed, just off shore, a lone surfer paddling around, desperately trying to catch a ride on a wind wave. It was a sorry sight to my eyes. I am also a surfer, but I get to enjoy much more favorable conditions than this desperate midwesterner. I live on the south coast of Australia, where, in contrast to the surface-level wind chop of Lake Michigan, we have a deep and powerful groundswell that comes from thousands of miles away in the deepest, remotest parts of the southern ocean. When the swell approaches our shores, you can see the sets of waves marching in from miles away like giant ripples from the horizon.

Wind waves are so called because the waves are immediately dependent on the wind. The waves last only as long as there is wind to produce them. But groundswell is at its most powerful when it is thousands of miles from the conditions that created it. The uninhibited journey that groundswell takes in open ocean gives it increasing momentum and power as it goes. We notice it most spectacularly when it approaches our coast. If we were out in the ocean, the groundswell would pass under us without us noticing more than a slight lift and fall of our vessel. But when it strikes land, it stands up majestically and peels and churns over reefs in a wondrous display of natural power. The spectacular sight we see on our shores is like the exuberant and energetic expression of joy in the jubilant psalms. The cause of this display, however, is to be found in a journey that began many miles away from the expression of jubilance itself.

As I said, wind waves depend on the immediate presence of wind to sustain them. When the wind stops, so do the waves. This shows that there is no real energy in the waves themselves. The energy is in the external atmosphere. So it is with superficial joy, an experience we sometimes remember as happiness. It gives us a taste of genuine happiness, but there is no energy in the experience itself. It is merely created by external circumstance, such as a relationship that makes us feel significant and valuable as long as the relationship lasts. But no sooner does the relationship end or the romance fade than the feeling dissipates, like wind waves when the weather moves on. In seeking happiness, we intuitively look to create immediate conditions that will yield immediate results. This gives us the sense that we are able to control and create our own happiness at will, but what we get is nothing more than wind chop.

The thrill of the rising and crashing waves of exuberant joy is a subject I will turn to later. At this point, however, I want to venture far away from the shore, where joy expresses itself in exuberance. I want to go far across the sea to where joy begins and where happiness is created. If you want more than a wind chop of joy in your life, I encourage you to follow me out into the deep water, into the featureless wasteland of the open ocean. Here something can be created in you, the momentum of which will not be dependent on the immediate conditions of your life at any one time. Like a great swell moving across the ocean from its deep source, your joy will attain a momentum that will endure through the uneventful moments when God seems distant. It will survive long periods of inactivity until God appears in its path and it crashes upon its destination with an abandonment of jubilance as it meets the one who is both its origin and its destination.

7

CREATIVE CONTRADICTIONS

Why, O LORD, do you stand far off?
Why do you hide yourself in times of trouble?

Psalm 10:1

Necessary Tension

The conditions that create joy are similar to those that create most forms of energy. Energy is created, generally speaking, in a situation of tension between elements. A storm, for example, develops when a low pressure system comes into contact with a high pressure system. One of the most interesting features of the psalms is the frequent, deliberate expression of the contradiction between divine revelation and reality. In many lament and supplicatory psalms, the psalmists expose and highlight the inconsistency between the declarations of God and their actual situation. In most cases, it is subtle and implied in the way the psalmist addresses God, but in other cases, it is more explicit, as in Psalm 44:

> You are my King and my God,
>   who decrees victories for Jacob.
> Through you we push back our enemies;
>   through your name we trample our foes.
> I do not trust in my bow,
>   my sword does not bring me victory;
> but you give us victory over our enemies,
>   you put our adversaries to shame.
> In God we make our boast all day long,
>   and we will praise your name forever.
>
> But now you have rejected and humbled us;
>   you no longer go out with our armies.

You made us retreat before the enemy,
    and our adversaries have plundered us.
You gave us up to be devoured like sheep
    and have scattered us among the nations.
You sold your people for a pittance,
    gaining nothing from their sale. (vv. 4–12)

In this psalm and others like it, the psalmist is dialing up the volume of the inherent tensions in his situation. He does this by upholding God's revelation of himself and his purposes, on the one hand, and the apparent circumstances surrounding him, on the other. In Psalm 44, the psalmist spends the first eight verses establishing how God has revealed his role as the protector of his people. After doing this, he then shows how starkly the present circumstances of the nation contradict this divine self-revelation.

There could be only two reasons for doing this: one being an expression of *unbelief* and the other being a profound expression of *faith*. A person might do this sort of thing to say, "See, this contradiction proves that God does not exist or does not care about us." But if that is not the psalmist's intent, then he is in fact saying, "This contradiction means that God is compelled, by his own self-revelation, to act in this situation." The unbeliever highlights the contradiction as an excuse to *not* believe. The believer highlights the contradiction as a way of exercising his faith. The latter is what we see taking place in the psalms. There were few things that Jesus delighted in more than when he saw people exercising their faith in this way. Let me give you an example.

The Prayer of Faith

One day, as Matthew tells us in his Gospel (15:21–28), a woman came to Jesus with a need. She cried out to Jesus to help her, believing that he could and would hear her even though she was a Gentile, a Phoenician (from the region of Tyre and Sidon) to be precise. Why did she believe the Jewish Messiah would help her? Simply because Jews practiced various laws that declared God's purpose to bless outsiders. It appears that she was aware of this, as would any poor foreigner who had visited Jewish areas. The Jews of Jesus's time apparently had lost sight of the meaning of these laws, but they were certainly very good at keeping laws for the sake of keeping laws. One of these laws was practiced by farmers in adherence to Leviticus 19:9–10, which stipulates:

> When you reap the harvest of your land, do not reap to the very edges of your field or gather the gleanings of your harvest. Do not go over your vineyard a second time or pick up the grapes that have fallen. Leave them for the poor and the alien. I am the LORD your God.

It seems that by observing this practice of the Jews, the Phoenician woman found some boldness to approach the Jewish Messiah. She saw in this law an expression of God's willingness to bless people like her. However, when she cried out to him, Matthew tells us that Jesus "did not answer a word" (v. 23). In other words, he ignored her! There was a tension, and she recognized it.

She could have responded to Jesus's silence with disillusionment, but she did the opposite. Rather than losing her faith, she exercised her faith in the exact kind of conditions where faith applies most poignantly. She kept following after Jesus and crying out to the point that the disciples urged Jesus to send her away. Such is the disturbance she created. But Jesus did this for a purpose. His silence was intentional. He wanted to draw out the faith of this woman and put it on display for all, including us, to see.

So Jesus turned to the woman and explained that he had come for his people, the Jews. But she was not deterred, because the tension fed her faith, and that faith was about to blossom. So she kept asking. Jesus then said something that drew her faith out into full flower. He said, "It is not right to take the children's bread and toss it to their dogs" (v. 26). To anyone without faith, this would have provided a final excuse to reject Jesus. But these words, for this woman, only served to intensify the tension so much that she burst out with an argument evidently alluding to the law in Leviticus 19:9. It is a spectacular moment and a compelling argument:

> "Yes, Lord," she said, "but even the dogs eat the crumbs that fall from their masters' table." (v. 27)

The Purpose of Prayer

Can we really argue with God? Yes, we can, and we must. If God knows what we need before we ask, as Jesus reminds us (see Matt. 6:8), then what is the point of praying? It is obviously not to tell God things he doesn't know. So why pray?

What God wants to see in prayer is *our willingness to trust in him*. In other words, he wants to see the reason for our prayer. He wants us to show him why we would come to him rather than trust solely in our own devices. Is our prayer just a token act of spirituality so that we feel we have "covered that base"? Is our prayer just a good luck ritual we perform to be successful in our own agendas?

True prayer demonstrates and *intensifies* faith. Faith is the willingness to entrust ourselves to God based on the conviction that God is faithful. When we make a case for why God should answer us, based on his self-revelation in Scripture, we demonstrate our conviction regarding God's faithfulness and also our willingness to trust him. The more we respond to the tension between God's promises and our situation by "arguing before the throne of grace" (as John Bunyan so aptly described it) in the manner demonstrated by the Phoenician woman, the more we will grow in faith and the more we will trust in God both now and in the future.

The faith that is *grown* in times of need is always far more precious a result than any answer to prayer we may have *received* as a result of the faith we demonstrated. The Phoenician woman received what she needed from God, but it was the faith that grew in her in the process of her pursuit that was the most important legacy of her encounter with Jesus. God wants to grow our faith because faith puts us where we belong, in God's hands. So it was that when the Phoenician woman finally revealed the reason for her insistence, that is, her belief in God's willingness to bless even an alien like her, Jesus was delighted. Jesus didn't just want this woman's grief and hardship to end; he wanted her alienation from God to end. As a result of her prayer, she ended up with both a healed daughter and a life repositioned into God's hands. That is what prayer is all about.

The Holy Argument

Now let's turn back to the Psalter, and we will see this sort of process unfolding in every context of supplication. The psalms, in fact, provide us with some key insights into the nature of prayer as God himself defines it. The most important element of the nature of the prayers in the psalms is their intensely *covenantal* tone. They are not formed in a vacuum and driven by need alone but rather are *evoked* by God's self-revelation. The approach that the psalmist takes is not that of a person who is pushed but of one who is *drawn*.

The context for prayer in the psalms is the implicit invitation given by God through his unconditional promise of favor and blessing for his people. The need creates the occasion for the psalmist to respond to this invitation and connect with the love of God.

It is important to note that the psalms do not present a process in which the psalmists arrive at a certain point by following certain steps. Rather, what takes place is a process in which God draws the individual into his love. We need to recognize the work of the Holy Spirit in the process, and in this sense also recognize the divine inspiration in the psalms. The psalms demonstrate what Paul refers to when he speaks of "praying in the Spirit" (Eph. 6:18). They are a remarkable foretaste, from an experience of a few prophetic authors, of what is now a possibility for us all. The psalms are God's perfect canonical example not just of what he wants *us* to do but also of what *he* wants to do within us.

A common feature of psalms of lament and supplication is the emergence of a remarkable outburst of praise from a covenant appeal as though the prayer were already answered (see Pss. 6; 13; 22; 28; 31; 54; 56; 57; 69; 71; 85; 109). It is not, however, that the circumstance has changed; the individual who prays has changed. The prayer of faith has brought him into an experiential connection with God's love, and it is here that faith blossoms into joy, irrespective of what the prevailing circumstances might be. The blossoming of faith is the creation of a bond between the individual and God. Not only is a desire met through this bond, but desire itself is also transformed. When desire is transformed, true happiness can be created, and joy can spring forth. Here is the process in Psalm 6:

The plea
O LORD, do not rebuke me in your anger
or discipline me in your wrath.

78

Be merciful to me, LORD, for I am faint;
O LORD, heal me, for my bones are in agony.
My soul is in anguish.
How long, O LORD, how long?

The covenant appeal
Turn, O LORD, and deliver me;
save me because of your unfailing love.
No one remembers you when he is dead.
Who praises you from the grave?

The lament
I am worn out from groaning;
all night long I flood my bed with weeping
and drench my couch with tears.
My eyes grow weak with sorrow;
they fail because of all my foes.

The exclamation of joy and praise
Away from me, all you who do evil,
for the LORD has heard my weeping.
The LORD has heard my cry for mercy;
the LORD accepts my prayer.
All my enemies will be ashamed and dismayed;
they will turn back in sudden disgrace. (vv. 1–10)

The covenant appeal that is made here is the most common appeal in the psalms. The psalmist appeals to God's *hesed*, a Hebrew word that has no exact equivalent in English (see Pss. 13:5; 31:16; 44:26; 51:1; 85:7; 119:41, 76; 130:7; 143:8). It is generally translated as "steadfast" or "unfailing love," though it is generally acknowledged to have strong covenantal overtones. It refers to God's love as expressed through his unconditional covenant. In appealing to God's *hesed*, the psalmist is upholding the covenant by which God bound himself to bless his people unconditionally (see also Ps. 83:3 in the light of Gen. 12:2).

This is followed by another appeal common in the psalms. It is an implicit appeal to God's expressed desire to be known for who he is—a loving and faithful God—and thereby glorified in all the earth. The psalmist argues the pointlessness of his demise in the light of this. His death would not cause God's name to be praised. Only his salvation could bring glory to God.

> No one remembers you when he is dead.
> Who praises you from the grave? (Ps. 6:5)

The same argument is made in Psalm 88:

> I call to you, O LORD, every day;
> I spread out my hands to you.
> Do you show your wonders to the dead?
> Do those who are dead rise up and praise you?
> Is your love declared in the grave,
> your faithfulness in Destruction?
> Are your wonders known in the place of darkness,
> or your righteous deeds in the land of oblivion?
> (vv. 9–12)

In Psalm 30, David testifies to having made this same kind of appeal:

> To you, O LORD, I called;
> to the Lord I cried for mercy:
> "What gain is there in my destruction,
> in my going down into the pit?
> Will the dust praise you?
> Will it proclaim your faithfulness?
> Hear, O LORD, and be merciful to me;
> O LORD, be my help." (vv. 8–10)

The tension that is often highlighted in appeals such as this is the tension between God's desire to be known and glorified as the one supreme sovereign Lord and the inevitable derision of the name of God that would occur should Israel be defeated by a foreign army. In the ancient Near East, a defeat in battle was not just seen as the defeat of an army but of a local deity. So when Israel was defeated in battle, the victors would lay derision on Israel's God. The Assyrian king does this in anticipation of winning a battle against Jerusalem in the time of Hezekiah, for example:

> Do not listen to Hezekiah, for he is misleading you when he says, "The LORD will deliver us." Has the god of any nation ever delivered his land from the hand of the king of Assyria? Where are the gods of Hamath and Arpad? Where are the gods of Sepharvaim, Hena and Ivvah? Have they rescued Samaria from my hand? Who of all the gods of these countries has been able to save his land from me? How then can the LORD deliver Jerusalem from my hand? (2 Kings 18:32–35)

Hezekiah feels this tension, and it underlies his prayer to God in this situation. Many of the laments that deal with foreign enemies also highlight this tension. Given that this kind of threat was the most common and most feared of all threats, it is not surprising to see this tension in so many psalms. Here are a couple of classic expressions of it:

> Help us, O God our Savior,
>   for the glory of your name;
> deliver us and forgive our sins
>   for your name's sake.
> Why should the nations say,
>   "Where is their God?" (Ps. 79:9–10)

But I am a worm and not a man,
 scorned by men and despised by the people.
All who see me mock me;
 they hurl insults, shaking their heads:
"He trusts in the LORD;
 let the LORD rescue him.
Let him deliver him,
 since he delights in him." (Ps. 22:6–8)

Relational Appeals

The appeals in the psalms find their historical precedent in both Abraham and Moses, the two men whose names are inextricably linked with the respective covenants they mediated (essentially the unfolding of the one covenant).

Abraham interceded for the evil populace of Sodom and Gomorrah among whom his nephew Lot lived. God's announcement to Abraham that he was about to destroy these cities was clearly designed to evoke the very kind of prayer that Abraham responded with on hearing this announcement:

> Then the LORD said, "Shall I hide from Abraham what I am about to do? Abraham will surely become a great and powerful nation, and all nations on earth will be blessed through him. For I have chosen him, so that he will direct his children and his household after him to keep the way of the LORD by doing what is right and just, so that the LORD will bring about for Abraham what he has promised him."
>
> Then the LORD said, "The outcry against Sodom and Gomorrah is so great and their sin so grievous that I will go down and see if what they have done is as bad as the outcry that has reached me. If not, I will know."
>
> The men turned away and went toward Sodom, but Abraham remained standing before the LORD. Then Abraham approached him and said: "Will you sweep away the righteous

with the wicked? What if there are fifty righteous people in the city? Will you really sweep it away and not spare the place for the sake of the fifty righteous people in it? Far be it from you to do such a thing—to kill the righteous with the wicked, treating the righteous and the wicked alike. Far be it from you! Will not the Judge of all the earth do right?"

The LORD said, "If I find fifty righteous people in the city of Sodom, I will spare the whole place for their sake." (Gen. 18:17–26)

In like manner, Moses prayed for his recalcitrant kinsmen after the exodus from Egypt when they made the golden calf.

"I have seen these people," the LORD said to Moses, "and they are a stiff-necked people. Now leave me alone so that my anger may burn against them and that I may destroy them. Then I will make you into a great nation."

But Moses sought the favor of the LORD his God. "O LORD," he said, "why should your anger burn against your people, whom you brought out of Egypt with great power and a mighty hand? Why should the Egyptians say, 'It was with evil intent that he brought them out, to kill them in the mountains and to wipe them off the face of the earth'? Turn from your fierce anger; relent and do not bring disaster on your people. Remember your servants Abraham, Isaac and Israel, to whom you swore by your own self: 'I will make your descendants as numerous as the stars in the sky and I will give your descendants all this land I promised them, and it will be their inheritance forever.'" Then the LORD relented and did not bring on his people the disaster he had threatened. (Exod. 32:9–14)

Abraham and Moses were the pioneers of intercessory prayer, and appropriately so, given that they both would subsequently be identified with the covenants God made with them. What they were doing in their prayers was applying the privileges that the covenant awarded to them. God had bound himself to his people by covenant, and Moses and Abraham were not slow to appeal to the very covenant of which God had made them mediators. Their prayers were enshrined as exemplary applications of the covenant and are therefore the historical precedents upon which the prayers of the psalms are based.

It is important that we see these appeals in the relational context to which they belong so that they don't appear as cold legal proceedings. The covenant itself that unfolds from Abraham to Moses and then consummates in Christ is intensely relational. It is more like a marriage contract than a business contract. The relational aspect of the covenant is overtly evident in the supplications of the psalms. Here the most common appeal is to the *character* of God and the self-appointed *role* of God in the lives of his people. In the psalms, the promises of God are simply an expression of the character of God. The tension that is most often highlighted in the psalms, therefore, is the tension between the psalmist's situation and the character of God.

One common example of this is the frequent appeal to God's justice in the psalms. The so-called imprecatory psalms (cursing psalms such as 14; 52; 58; 59; etc.) can be sorely misunderstood if they are not understood within this context. They are not just expressions of hatred; they express the tension that exists because of injustice. Jesus tells us to love our enemies because of the injustice inherent in one sinful person judging another sinful person. He is therefore forbidding personal vengeance. The imprecatory psalms do not contradict this. They are not expressions of personal vengeance but of a desire for the vengeance of God to right injustice. In this sense, the imprecatory psalms are anticipating final judgment and declaring, in God's name, the verdict of God upon those who persist in evil ways.

Where hatred toward people is expressed in the psalms, and it *is* expressed in the psalms (see Ps. 139:21), it has a formal context in which a person is not hated *personally* but by virtue of what they represent in that formal context. It is the same in a war when a soldier defends his own by shooting at an enemy soldier. This act of hatred is not an act of personal hatred against the individual soldier but against what that soldier represents in the formal context of the war. The focus of the hatred in the psalms is always on the evil scheme being represented by the enemy. The issue being highlighted is the way in which this evil scheme contradicts the purpose of God. The expressions of anger in the psalms are therefore expressions of a felt tension between God's justice and the deeds of people.

> For you are not a God who delights in wickedness;
>> evil may not dwell with you. . . .
> For there is no truth in their mouth;
>> their inmost self is destruction;
> their throat is an open grave;
>> they flatter with their tongue.
> Make them bear their guilt, O God;
>> let them fall by their own counsels;
> because of the abundance of their transgressions cast
>> them out,
>> for they have rebelled against you. (Ps. 5:4, 9–10
>> ESV)

> How long will the wicked, O LORD,
>> how long will the wicked be jubilant?
> They pour out arrogant words;
>> all the evildoers are full of boasting.
> They crush your people, O LORD;
>> they oppress your inheritance.
> They slay the widow and the alien;
>> they murder the fatherless.

They say, "The LORD does not see;
    the God of Jacob pays no heed." . . .
Does he who disciplines nations not punish?
    (Ps. 94:3–7, 10)

The Seedbed of Joy

In summary, in the lament psalms, even in the most seemingly despairing ones, the psalmists deliberately bring two things into tension. They deliberately highlight the reality of their situation as it stands in tension with the reality of God and his promises. As both realities are amplified, this very tension then becomes the seedbed for faith and hope. Faith is conceived by the injection of the divine promise into the open wound of a heart that has allowed itself to be wounded by reality.

Faith is the gesture of entrusting ourselves to the certainty of what God has promised even though we do not yet see it realized. Hope is the longing for the object of faith's belief. Hope compels us to seek, and it is by seeking that we open our hearts to receive God. This becomes the source of our joy.

In Romans 5, Paul says, "We rejoice in the hope of the glory of God" (v. 2). As we seek God, in other words, we receive a deposit of what is to come: by the Holy Spirit, the glory of God begins to dawn in our hearts (v. 5). So if *hope* is the source of our joy, how then is hope formed within us? Here Paul echoes the principle I have identified as central in the spirituality of the psalms. He says, "Suffering produces perseverance; perseverance, character; and character, hope" (vv. 3–4). In other words, suffering, by producing hope, opens the door for us to know true joy.

I hasten to add, though, that suffering itself does not automatically produce hope. Suffering can put us in touch with reality if we allow ourselves to both realize that reality and *persevere* in seeking God through that reality. If we *persevere*, we will develop a rightly oriented *character*, and a person with a rightly oriented character is one whose desires are oriented toward God and his will. I will discuss this process more in the next chapter, so suffice it to say now that the orientation of our desires is the key to happiness and the source of joy.

I am conscious of the fact that this all sounds a little academic. None of this is easy. If there is anything I would want you to take away from this discussion, it is that you have permission to struggle in hardship. We can tend to think that faith only ever sees the positive and that it is somehow an abandonment of faith to acknowledge our hardship. This is a common misconception about faith spawned by influences outside Scripture. The Bible teaches us that, on the contrary, faith itself grows out of the tension between divine promise and worldly reality.

We must acknowledge our tendency to want to resolve this tension by either downplaying the promises of God or downplaying reality. People can go either way. The positive-thinking movement in Christendom has fallen into the latter category by erroneously defining faith, in effect, as the abandonment of reality. But the tendency to make the opposite error is much more common in Christian circles, that is, to resolve the tension between divine promise and worldly reality by downplaying the promises of God. We downplay the promises of God when we subtly lower our expectations of God. There are many ways to make lowered expectations look biblical, but they all fly in the face of an abundant and clear testimony in Scripture to the opposite.

It is difficult to maintain high expectations of God when God seems so distant, and it is tempting to try to make excuses for God in the name of faith. When we justify lowered expectations, however, we only erode faith because faith arises from the very tension we find so awkward. As demonstrated here, the psalmists never played down the tension between the divine promises and the reality of their situations. On the contrary, they highlighted this tension and intensified their sense of it. As a result, their faith sprang forth with joyful expressions of confidence.

8

THE WAITING ROOM

Wait for the LORD;
  be strong and take heart
  and wait for the LORD.

Psalm 27:14

The Long Wait

Waiting. It is the most common experience portrayed in the psalms. It is largely implicit, but it forms the context for much of what the psalmists expressed. Occasionally, they provided an explicit expression of it, as when the psalmist cries out in vexation, "How long, O LORD, how long?" (Psalm 6:3; 13:1; 35:17; 74:9–10; 89:46; 90:13; 94:3; 119:84). Waiting is the underlying experience behind every psalm that reaches out for God in some way, whether in grief or in joy. The seeming absence of God is the most common theme of grief in the lament psalms. The other common theme of grief regards evil and injustice, where the implied question is, "*When* is God going to bring justice on the earth?" Many of the psalms that declare God's faithfulness and goodness for his people were written to help people wait patiently and confidently for God in times when the memories of his mighty deeds were receding into the distant past. Likewise, many of the expressions of thanks and praise were the psalmists' endeavors to bolster their waning hope.

Waiting is in fact what we see God's people doing for most of biblical history. Of course, we tend not to notice this aspect of the story. What draws our attention is the series of amazing acts of God on behalf of his people. What we tend to miss, however, are the long spaces of time in between these acts of God. Most of the history recorded in the Bible is not made up of sensational acts of God. Most of the biblical history consists of people waiting for God to do something. And often they waited in very dire circumstances that made the wait all the more difficult. They were held in the tension between the divine promise and the seeming absence of any implementation of that promise.

Throughout the book of Psalms, the mighty acts of God are celebrated, but it is important to note that most of the psalms were written in the gaps, in the periods *when God wasn't doing anything.* They are prayers, poems of longing, and songs of praise composed in the uninspiring chambers of life's waiting room. This is undoubtedly why these songs were seen to be so pertinent by those who compiled the Psalter as we have it today.

As I have pointed out, the Psalter was compiled into its final edition after the Jewish exile in Babylon. The exiles returned to Jerusalem with high hopes, expecting to see the grand visions of Daniel, Jeremiah, and Isaiah fulfilled. They had waited in exile for many decades, and now it seemed that the time of fulfillment was at hand. It *was* a time of fulfillment, but not what they expected. It was really only a transition to the next period of waiting. It is like when you are moved from a hospital waiting room to a cubicle, where you wait in greater anticipation, though often for much longer than you did in the official waiting room.

This next period of waiting would be the longest and in some ways the most painful of all the periods of Israel's waiting. It was more painful because the people saw themselves as generally more devoted than before, and yet they experienced a period of prophetic silence without parallel in length since the time of Abraham. In other words, the tension between the divine promise and the reality of their situation was never as intense as it was now. In this context, the psalms comforted them and helped them to persevere. When they read David's prayers, they found in this model man of faith an experience with which they could identify. So they gathered his psalms and others to help them in their time of unfulfilled hopes. The psalms helped them wait in their own context of life's waiting room.

The Convoluted Path

Many of David's psalms were written during his painful fugitive years when, though having been given the divine promise of kingship, he lived as an exile, often in caves in the desert. The agony of David's wait lay largely in the fact that the kingship promised to him by God had seemed so imminent. He had been anointed by God's prophet, and he had defeated Israel's enemy. These were the customary steps into kingship, but they had not landed him where he had expected. His ship to royalty, so to speak, was pulling into the harbor of its destination only then to be swept far out to sea. He felt, as Psalm 22 expresses, completely forsaken by God. Why would God dangle this promise before him and bring him to such close proximity to its fulfillment only to thrust him away from it? This is the question that has burned in the heart of every person who has had the shore of their God-given dreams within reach only to find themselves locked in a current going out to sea in the opposite direction.

If you feel you are being tossed around on a stormy ocean, going farther out to sea without any sign of a destination, then you are in the place where many of the psalms were written. In fact, as I have said, it is the place where most of the road of biblical history was laid. Abraham waited for his promised son for fourteen years. Joseph received the covenant promise of favor only to suffer in slavery and languish in a putrid Egyptian dungeon for fourteen years. And if you think this is bad, think about the generations of Israelites who suffered in slavery in Egypt. Moses was obviously keen to take action for his enslaved kinsmen (Exod. 2:12), but he would have to spend forty years herding goats in the desert before God turned up and called him to do something.

The compounding difficulty in these situations was the painful incongruence between the urgency of the situation and the apparent slowness of God to act. In situations such as these, we imagine God sitting back apathetically with his head turned the other way. This was the experience of the Canaanite woman who pleaded with Jesus to heal her daughter only to be met with silence and, evidently, a turned back. The questions that arise within us in times such as these are, "Why doesn't God care? Why has God rejected me? Why has he turned away from me?"

Some people will, at this point, insist that we should get our attention off our vacillating feelings and focus on the facts of the situation. The last thing we should do, they suppose, is to give any validity to fickle feelings. This sounds noble, but it is intensely antirelational. If my wife communicates to me her troubled feelings about our relationship and I respond by dismissing her feelings in this way, I would be well on my way to shipwrecking our relationship. Relationships are built on communication, and communication is possible only when feelings are freely expressed, heard, and validated.

This is what we see in the psalms. The psalms are deeply relational expressions of how people felt; few of them were ever meant to be objective analyses of how things really were. The psalms, however, are more than just poems to express feelings for the sake of expression itself. They are directed to a person, to the person of God.

Time to Seek

Why does God make us wait? Obviously, some things should come only at the right time, and therefore trusting that God knows the right time and being prepared to wait for the right time are elementary. But some things are *always* right for us to have. No child of God should ever be content with just an abstract knowledge of God. We must always reach out for God to impact our experience. In the psalms, people look for God to manifest himself in their situation. They know God is there in an objective sense. What they want is for God to impact and transform their present experience. It is always right to want this.

Paul tells us to be filled with the Holy Spirit as an ongoing, repeated experience (Eph. 5:18), and Jesus tells us that God will certainly give his Holy Spirit to those who ask (Luke 11:13). Yet any seasoned pilgrim of the spiritual life knows that there are periods in which we long and pray for the outpouring of God's Spirit and receive no immediate answer. It seems that Jesus's words, though true, do not promise *immediacy*. The psalms are testimony to the fact that, while people cry out for the embrace of God, God nevertheless deliberately holds off for no other apparent reason than to extend the period of waiting itself. So again, why the waiting?

What the psalms highlight is the fact that there is significant value in the process of waiting itself before any response from God is considered. This waiting is not a passive and inactive state. It is intensely active. It involves longing, anticipating, yearning. It is *seeking*. It is, in other words, the exercising of one's desire for God. Expression of desire is vital to relationship. That God would give us time to express our desire for him is entirely understandable in a relational context. In a relationship, there is as much importance in mutual desire for togetherness as there is in the fulfillment of that desire. My wife will say to me, "I don't just want an appointment in your diary. I want you to *want* to be with me." God wants us to *want him*, and he gives us time to allow this desire to emerge and grow. He doesn't just want servants to do what he says. He wants children who will reciprocate his love. He wants us to delight in him.

Seeking is the greatest expression of praise and worship. By persistently seeking God, we declare that he is supremely desirable. To seek God is to glorify God, that is, to declare his supreme worth. We might declare with our lips that God is worthy of all praise, but we demonstrate what is truly worth the most to us by what we *pursue*. The psalms in which people seek God, even from the most alienated positions, are truly psalms of praise and worship, perhaps even more so than those that explicitly make declarations of praise and worship.

> As the deer pants for streams of water,
>   so my soul pants for you, O God.
> My soul thirsts for God, for the living God.
>   When can I go and meet with God? (Ps. 42:1–2)

> O God, you are my God,
>   earnestly I seek you;
> my soul thirsts for you,
>   my body longs for you,
> in a dry and weary land
>   where there is no water.

> I have seen you in the sanctuary
>   and beheld your power and your glory.

> Because your love is better than life,
>   my lips will glorify you. (Ps. 63:1–3)

Let us note that these psalms were written by troubled people who felt alienated from God. In their alienation, it seems that their desire for God was awakened, their hearts were reoriented toward their goal, and faith was exercised and increased.

As a desire for God grows in our hearts, all those other desires that exercise such tyranny over our lives are conquered, and the heart is liberated and consecrated to God. I will describe this remarkable process in the next chapter.

9

THE LIBERATION
OF DESIRE

Delight yourself in the LORD
and he will give you the desires of your heart.

Psalm 37:4

The Power of Desire

Our desires determine our lives. We will always pursue and act according to what we desire the most in any moment. Rational thought has no power over desire. A heroin addict knows that heroin will ruin his life, but he still injects it into his veins. No amount of rational dissuasion will change this. Why? Because we always follow the strongest desire we have in any moment. The way to escape a destructive desire is not to try to deny the desire. This never works. We can overcome one desire only with another greater desire. Where one desire clashes with another, the greater desire will turn the lesser desire into repulsion precisely because it threatens the greater desire.

Many people claim to want to know God, but because they have a greater desire for something that they intuitively know God will challenge, they inevitably shield themselves from God. This process is rarely obvious and most often subconscious. It is not uncommon for people to be vexed at God's seeming absence from them when in fact it is they who are subconsciously defending themselves against God. The solution to this scenario is first of all to make ourselves conscious of what we really desire. But even when we are conscious of what we desire, it is impossible to change that desire just by self-will. How do we change what we want when we want what we want more than we want to change?

We cannot break out of this cycle without some external intervention. Thankfully, God provides that external help. He breaks the cycle of desire by downloading his desires directly into our hearts, as God said through Ezekiel: "I will put my Spirit in you and move you to follow my decrees and be careful to keep my laws" (Ezek. 36:27). What the Holy Spirit delivers to our hearts with his indwelling presence is a *choice*. We are now able to choose one desire over another, and the desire we choose is the one that will grow.

In every seeking psalm, the psalmist chooses one desire over another. He chooses to be dependent on God over his propensity to independently solve his own problems. When David declares his famous "one thing I ask" prayer, he is not only exercising the desire for God that had taken hold of his heart but also willing that desire to increasingly overpower his heart and become preeminent. This is an expression of the reorientation of desire that is taking place in his situation of hardship. David's desire itself is being reoriented toward its intended goal:

> One thing I ask of the LORD,
>   this is what I seek:
> that I may dwell in the house of the LORD
>   all the days of my life,
> to gaze upon the beauty of the LORD
>   and to seek him in his temple. (Ps. 27:4)

The Purpose of Desire

We were created in the image of God, which, among other things, means that we were created as relational beings.

Relationships are therefore the fulfillment of our being—first our relationship with God and then by natural consequence with our fellow humans. This is the context for which desire was intended. We were created to desire that which fulfills our being. The result of disconnection from God is therefore also the disorientation of desire. Once we are disconnected from God, desires focus on *objects* rather than on relationships. In our dysfunction, we still relate to people, but we have a tendency to relate to them as objects rather than as subjects.

This is not always completely the case because the divine image remains in us even if it is greatly marred. But the dysfunction is evident in all people to some extent. It is evident when we choose friends who make us feel good about ourselves by association. It is evident when a man leaves his wife because she is no longer as attractive as she was. It is evident when a parent rejects a son or daughter because of disappointment over what he or she has become. In these ways, we reduce "personhood" to the sum of certain qualities and turn persons into objects. The desire for objects flows from the basic original desire in the first human beings to be more than what they were; hence, they first objectified themselves. From that time on, people have pursued objects in their quest for greater identity.

Desire, however, was meant for relationships. To sustain relationships, desire must have the quality of never being satisfied with having achieved an objective. This is how it should be because relationships are not objectives and people are not objects. Desire is insatiable precisely so that we can never say of a relationship, "I am satisfied now, and I don't feel any more desire to keep loving and pursing this relationship to greater depths." The insatiability of desire is meant to perpetuate love. I love my children. I love to be with them and to hug them and kiss them. My desire to do this, moreover, is never satisfied; it never fades by having enough time together and enough hugs and kisses. I never feel like I have given and received enough love. This is the wonderful thing about the role that desire plays in its right context. The perpetual nature of desire gives me continual joy in my relationships with those whom I love.

When we transfer desire onto *objects*, however, then the insatiable nature of desire throws us into a torturous cycle of discontent. When we desire wealth, fame, and success, when we desire people as sexual objects or as sources for our own identity validation, when we desire power and influence, these desires will become a source of great sorrow rather than joy. We will find ourselves in an endless cycle of painful discontent. What makes this worse is that the more we set our desires on objects, the less able we will be to sustain relationships. The relational void then creates a vacuum in our souls that will make our unsatisfied desires all the more painful and our gratified desires all the less satisfying. This in turn serves to further perpetuate the painful cycle.

To escape this cycle, we need God to intervene, and this is what God does. As I have said, we cannot overcome desires on our own. What we desire is what we desire; we cannot *not* desire what we desire. When God places his desires within us by his Spirit, this gives us a choice. We have a choice to exercise either the desire of our dysfunctional nature or the desire of the Holy Spirit within us. In the light of this new option, the apostle Paul exhorts us in his letter to the Galatians, saying, "Live by the Spirit, and you will not gratify the desires of the sinful nature" (5:16). Paul also says in his Epistle to the Romans, "Those who live according to the sinful nature have their minds set on what that nature desires; but those who live in accordance with the Spirit have their minds set on what the Spirit desires" (8:5).

The desire of the Spirit is no mystery. It is well documented in Scripture and explicitly stated. It is for *relationship*. God wants a relationship with us in the context of a broader family relationship. He wants us to love him and to love those whom he loves. This is of course what Jesus identified as the greatest commandment: "Love the Lord your God with all your heart and with all your soul and with all your mind and with all your strength." And flowing from this, "Love your neighbor as yourself" (Mark 12:30–31).

Desire belongs in relationship because relationship is God's desire. He desires relationship with us, and therefore to be aligned with all reality and truth, we must reciprocate this desire. This is what is happening in the psalms that express an insatiable longing for God. The psalmists are simply reciprocating God's desire for them. When desire focuses on relationships, we fulfill the very nature of our created being. As we desire God, we begin to desire God's desires, we begin to value God's values, and we begin to love those whom God loves. "Delight yourself in the LORD," says the psalmist, "and he will give you the desires of your heart" (37:4).

When we desire God above all, then all other things can be enjoyed for what they are. We will actually find greater joy in the pleasures of life because we no longer need these pleasures to fill the vacuum left by the absence of God. And so the desire for God does not equate with asceticism. When we delight in God, we have a greater capacity to take pleasure in the pleasures of life. God created all things for our pleasure, *not* to be the fulfillment of our deepest desires.

Cultivating Desire

Desire is like a muscle. The more we exercise it, the more it grows. We exercise a desire by seeking the object of our desire. So if we desire wealth, for example, then the more we seek wealth, the more our desire for it will grow. The more we anticipate being wealthy, the more we fantasize about the wealthy life, and every time we make a decision based on this desire, the desire grows to the point where we will even begin to sacrifice relationships for the desire (even, and especially, our relationship with God). But the same principle applies to seeking God. The more we seek God, the more our desire for God will grow. And if we keep on seeking God, if we refuse to give up until we have found God and even then keep seeking a deeper knowledge of God, if we stubbornly persist in seeking God in the face of all doubt and discouragement, then our desire for God will gradually outgrow our other desires.

As this happens, all our other desires will be subsumed under the primary desire for God. In this way, desire finds its purpose and everything will come into alignment in our hearts. It is not that we should not desire other things, but we should not allow other things to become more important to us than our relationship with God. When our relationship with God is our highest value, we will be able to enjoy other things for what they are. If we value our relationship with God above all other relationships, we will be liberated to love people and receive love from people without needing them to provide that vital and unique identity-giving love that only God can provide. When we love God *as God*, that is, as Lord of our hearts, then we are able to love people *as people*.

Here is the importance of waiting for God. Here is why God gives us time, lots of time, to seek before we find. By seeking God, we exercise our desire for God, and as we exercise our desire for God, it grows. And when our desire for God grows to a place of supremacy in our hearts, then God is truly the God of our hearts. Seeking, therefore, creates within us the capacity to know God *as God*. It is by seeking that we are able to find God because seeking enables our hearts to receive God. If we don't desire God above all things, then we are still blind to God. God cannot be known *and* depreciated. To know God is to know his supreme worthiness. To know God is to desire him above all. The more we cultivate a desire for God, the more our hearts are able to know him for who he is.

Patience

We are an impatient lot, we postmodern technophiles. We get everything so quickly, at the push of a button or the click of a mouse, and so we have largely lost the ability to wait. When we call on God, we expect him to turn up right away with our requests in hand, but from where has this expectation come? It is a culturally formed expectation, not a biblically formed one. The biblical narrative—and particularly the psalms—show us that God often allows a lot of time between the seeking and the finding so as to intensify the seeking, which in turn enlarges the finding. But when we call out to God, if we don't get an answer, if we don't sense his peace and joy right away, we tend to give up and go away disillusioned. Our desires have been so overindulged that they are easily exhausted by expending the smallest effort in pursuit of anything. Easy pleasure and constant entertainment of the senses have immobilized our will against pursuing anything beyond arm's reach.

It is time to get fit again. If God puts us down and walks a hundred yards away, it is because he wants to teach us how to run. He wants us to exercise our desire for him until with all our being we know that he is all we need. God holds out the psalms to us as a standard of earnestness so that these expressions of desire for God will become a running track on which our fattened souls can be exercised.

To step onto this track is to step into the flow of the Spirit's yearning within us that draws us forward into the love of God. As we run this race, in step with the Spirit, we will find our spiritual capacities invigorated. That deeply suppressed childlike yearning for divine fatherly love will awaken within us and will compel our desires forward with an ever-increasing energy. It is as though the heart were a solar-powered rocket destined for the sun whose speed increases as it moves closer to its destination precisely because its destination is also the source of its energy. The more we seek God, the greater our desire for God will become, and the more passionate our pursuit of God will become. In this way, our spirits will be awakened and our hearts liberated to desire what desire itself was made for.

> I am still confident of this:
>   I will see the goodness of the LORD
>   in the land of the living.
> Wait for the LORD;
>   be strong and take heart
>   and wait for the LORD. (Ps. 27:13–14)

10

THE HAPPIEST MAN

Surely I have calmed and quieted my soul,
like a weaned child with his mother;
like a weaned child is my soul within me.

Psalm 131:2 NKJV

The Joy of Needing God

Joy is liberated desire. Happiness is not found in the satisfaction of many conflicting desires but in the fulfillment of desire itself. The will must be drawn into the orbit that stabilizes it in its intended path. It must lock itself into the gravitational pull of God and allow itself to orbit forever around him. "I shall not want," says David in the most well known of all the psalms. Why? Because "The LORD is my shepherd" (Ps. 23:1). He is not just celebrating the continual providence of God. His other psalms demonstrate the depth of his intention here. David's needs were indeed met by God, but when he lacked everything else that one might desire in life, he found the most profound joy in God.

The highest moments of happiness in the psalms are not found in the exuberant praise psalms but in the psalms that are clearly written in times of severe vulnerability and need. These were moments of profound discovery. Here we see the breakdown of the whole edifice of worldly success serving to drive the hearts of David and the other psalmists to God and to help them discover something about themselves that becomes eternally liberating. It is the discovery of the simplicity of human desire. All we need in life is God. The most ineffably profound enjoyment possible for the human soul is the embrace of God. To be filled with God, to be enfolded by the parental love of God, to become the manifestation of the mission of God is the consummate fulfillment of all that desire was created to pursue.

As an old Spanish proverb says, "The richest man is not the one who has the most but the one who needs the least." The happiest man, in other words, is not the one who has the most of what disoriented warring desires demand but the one who has reoriented desire itself. The happiest man is the one who needs nothing but God, who refuses to live without God, who says, "If God does not go with me into life, then it is no life at all, whatever I may have or achieve."

The Superstition of Materialism

When most people think of being happy, they think of a set of circumstances that they believe will create this happiness. This association is based on past experiences in which a change in circumstances or the attainment of certain things provided an experience of joy. The problem is that, once we become accustomed to a set of circumstances or the possession of certain things, this joy fades.

I will never forget our excitement when my wife and I moved into our house. It is a well-designed house but quite small compared to many of the houses around us, and it was very cheaply built. But it felt like a luxurious palace to us. We were so giddy with joy on the first night that we just sat in the main room soaking up the atmosphere like lizards in the sun. A few years ago, I considered buying a piece of land just down the road and building a bigger house. We have three children, and I felt we needed more space. There was nothing morally wrong with this choice in itself, but my reasons for making the choice were seriously flawed. I thought that life would be better for me and my family in a bigger house. Why else would we go to the trouble of taking on a building project and moving?

My first doubts were aroused by the evidence from family experience. My wife is one of four siblings who were brought up in a tiny house in Geelong, Australia. The children shared small rooms, and they were very happy children. For a time, my family lived in a small cottage in the bush. My father, a hardworking German immigrant who does everything himself, built it out of trees that he had cut down and milled. It had two rooms and a loft. It was a wonderful and happy time of my life, and my parents would agree with this. So we decided our children would not suffer for having to share a room. But there was a deeper error at work in my thinking.

In wanting a bigger and better house, I was responding to an automated desire to find happiness by manipulating my environment. I held the mistaken notion that a change in my external circumstances would somehow change my inner spiritual state, resulting in my happiness. This is akin to superstition; it certainly is no more logical than any other superstitious belief. People may attribute the disasters of a day to the fact that they walked under a ladder in the morning or saw a black cat. Or they may attribute their successes to an amulet they wear around their neck or the fact that they knocked on wood when they made their plans. We call it superstition because there is no real connection between these external objects and circumstances.

The media constantly preaches the superstition of materialism. We get the message that if we have the right home and car, wear the right clothes, have a nice-looking partner, have the right job, and achieve the right level of success and admiration, then we will be happy. This is no better than thinking that wearing an amulet will bring me luck. These objects and objectives are of no more significance in and of themselves than if they were large empty boxes arranged around us in combinations said to be magically effective. The thought that changing my job, house, and partner will bring me happiness is no different from thinking that facing my desk the other way will make me more intelligent. The external furniture of our lives has no immediate logical relationship to our inward state of happiness.

I should hasten to add that I am not proposing a dualistic view of life in which everything inward and spiritual is good and everything material is bad. There is no such dualism in Scripture. The material universe is significant and good. That is clear from the first chapter of Genesis. But the significance of creation has to do with its role in the relationship between God and man. Rather than thinking that creation is only the *context* in which God relates to humans, we need to view the significance of creation *within* the relationship between God and humans. Creation is the expression of God's attributes. God loves to bless his people with things that give them pleasure. Creation is a relational gesture made to celebrate and express the bond of love between God and humans. In this sense, material things are indeed connected with our happiness inasmuch as they are experienced within the relational context. Material things have no value in themselves anymore than a one-dollar bill has any intrinsic value (it is just a bit of paper with certain markings on it).

According to the Bible, and I am thinking of the first two chapters of Genesis in particular, material things are the currency of a relational interchange. God enjoys his creation with his children, and he enjoys their enjoyment. It is all part of a relational experience. If we are blessed with wealth, the only way this can lead to happiness is if it leads us to recognize God's goodness to us in entrusting such resources to our stewardship. It is not the wealth that creates the happiness but the relational connection that is celebrated through the gift of wealth.

Let's go back to me and my house. I now enjoy this house more than ever; in fact, I would say it contributes to whatever degree of happiness I have. This is not because my house has changed but because *my experience* of it has changed. Discontentment in our affluent world is not caused by lack but by comparison. This is why we keep buying new televisions. The new models make the old models look bad even though the last model looked amazing to us when we first bought it. I realized that I was experiencing my house in the wrong way. Actually, to be precise, I wasn't experiencing my house at all. I was constantly thinking about what I *could* have, not what I *did* have. I was robbing myself of the enjoyment of what I had by constantly reaching for what I didn't have. Why do we do this? This is an important question, and it leads me to the point I want to make here.

The Externalization of Renewal

Our obsession with material upgrades is, I believe, simply the externalization of our need for constant spiritual-relational renewal. I have said that desire was made for relationships. It is therefore of such a nature as to never be satisfied with any static goal. I must never get to the point where I say of God or another person, "I have had enough of you now and no longer feel the need to keep seeking an ever-deepening enjoyment of our togetherness." A relationship is perpetuated precisely because we always desire a deeper experience of togetherness. A relationship is healthy and alive only when it is growing. Given that our relationships are an integral part of our selfhood (I am truly myself only when I am in a right

115

relationship with God and others), as long as our relationships are being constantly renewed and are growing, then we ourselves are being renewed and are growing. That which does not grow is dying or dead.

We therefore have a deep, inner need for constant spiritual-relational renewal, and this need is fulfilled by a constant engagement with, and enjoyment of, our relationship with God first and other people second. We feel renewed and invigorated as we renew and grow these relationships. If, however, we detach ourselves from our relationships, if we disconnect from God and begin to objectify other people, we will lack this sense of renewal and will inevitably try to create this sense of newness by renewing the externals of our lives. We will be constantly swapping one object for another in the belief that the change of objects will magically effect a state of spiritual newness within us.

Of course, much is legitimate about the desire to renew the circumstances of our lives. Life is legitimately more interesting when we change things up now and again: a new color for the house, a new look in the wardrobe, and even a new occupation. All this is a good and natural part of enjoying life. The problem is that we often renew our circumstances to fill the painful lack of renewal and growth in our relationships with God and others. Our deepest spiritual need is for relationship, first relationship with God and then relationship with others. Imagine being the only person left on earth. You get to inherit everything that humans have ever made, but you are alone. I assure you that the deep, painful loneliness would render every material benefit absolutely void. Material things have worth only in the context of the basic relational interchanges of vital, growing relationships.

If we feel stagnant, dissatisfied, and empty, we must understand that changing our external circumstances will not make us happier in the long term. That is something that the collective experience of human beings has verified over and over again. It is common wisdom, and it is spelled out in the Bible. The immediate pleasure of new circumstances or objects may disguise the emptiness, but it will not take it away. What we need to do is what the psalmists constantly did: We need to renew our relationship with God.

It is painfully simple but ultimately true. When we get ourselves into a momentum of relational renewal with God, then everything else comes into alignment. We are then able to relate to other people *as people*, without their having to fill the void that the absence of God creates in our hearts. And when our relationships are in order, then we find that material things can be enjoyed for what they are. Objects then find their rightful place in the context of relationship, and we begin to experience them differently. So rather than changing our circumstances, we will have changed the way we experience our circumstances. This is the key.

One more word about my house. When I understood these things, I was able to see my house differently. When I walk through the gate, I see a monument to the goodness of God. I see his providence in every beam and stone. The house is like a message from God to me, a message of his faithfulness and care for me and my family. My house has meaning for me only in the context of my relationships. I am satisfied with my house because I am satisfied in my God, who has provided this house for me. Money will build me a bigger house, but only my relationships with God, my wife, and my children can provide me with a sense of home. So if I am going to put effort into building something, I will expend that effort on building my relationships first, for when my relationships grow, I am renewed and so is my experience of everything else in life.

Noncontingent Joy

It is a remarkable feature of the psalms that expressions of joy are often entirely incongruent with the circumstances from which the psalms arise. External circumstances make the psalmists anxious and throw them into grief, but it is not the change in these circumstances that makes them happy. They often express genuine joy before anything changes. They express joy in times of abundance and pleasure and, with equal and sometimes greater intensity, in times of hardship and loss, demonstrating that external circumstances have very little to do with the attainment of happiness. The only necessary connection between the two in the psalms is when loss drives the psalmists to a new discovery of God or when thanksgiving reestablishes a former connection with God. Either way, the external circumstances do not create the happiness. Rather, the external circumstances are simply a tool of revelation and guidance as God seeks to draw his people back into his embrace.

Sometimes the psalmists get what they plead for and sometimes they don't, but in both cases, the process of seeking God shapes their desires into something different from what they initially thought they wanted from God. The change is not always dramatic. Often just the reestablishment of the psalmist's relationship with God brings the aching of his unfulfilled desire into a calm state of orbit. He still needs what he needs, be it provision or protection or whatever else he has pleaded for. But the process of seeking God has lifted his gaze to something higher. His desires have locked onto something infinitely more attractive than any material thing. He has reconnected with the love of God, and in doing so, he has rediscovered his sonship. The love of God has lifted him up to the level of existence for which human beings were created. He is no longer just concerned about subsistence, health, and protection to keep himself and his people alive. He has been reawakened to the purpose of life itself. There are many examples of this movement in the psalms, but I think the greatest example is found in Psalm 73.

The Journey to Happiness

Psalm 73 is a valuable example of the reorientation of desire because it depicts the entire journey in retrospect for didactic purposes. It is essentially a wisdom psalm in the tradition of the book of Job. This retrospective objectivity helps us to more clearly map a journey that is played out in the subjective expressions of the other psalms.

In accord with all the complaints and supplications in the Psalter, the psalmist, let's say it is Asaph (to whom this psalm is attributed in the title), highlights a *tension*. It is the tension between God's promise of blessing to those who walk in his ways and the obvious fact of his own seemingly inexplicable suffering. The main source of his psychological misery in this situation, however, was not his hardships but the disorientation of his desire. He was unable to feel the consoling warmth of God's goodness because his desires had been hijacked by envy. He coveted the material wealth of the godless rich. He saw them being satisfied by the gratification of their every desire, and he felt this to be the happiness he longed for. He envied the security of the sheltered existence they were able to build for themselves with their wealth. He felt that the God who had promised happiness to his people was not being faithful to him and not being just.

> Surely God is good to Israel,
>> to those who are pure in heart.

But as for me, my feet had almost slipped;
    I had nearly lost my foothold.
For I envied the arrogant
    when I saw the prosperity of the wicked.

They have no struggles;
    their bodies are healthy and strong.
They are free from the burdens common to man;
    they are not plagued by human ills. . . .

This is what the wicked are like—
    always carefree, they increase in wealth. (Ps. 73:1–
        5, 12)

Asaph tells how this tension nearly caused him to lose faith. But, as we see, it was in this tension that his faith was awakened. Like a bodybuilder straining to make that last bench press, he kept upholding the tension before God until at last there was a breakthrough. Where it seems that faith was being weakened by the strain, it was in fact being strengthened by the exertion. The final burst of strength in his faith took him into the temple, where he had an encounter with God that is left undescribed, most probably because it was indescribable.

Surely in vain have I kept my heart pure;
    in vain have I washed my hands in innocence.
All day long I have been plagued;
    I have been punished every morning.

If I had said, "I will speak thus,"
    I would have betrayed your children.
When I tried to understand all this,
    it was oppressive to me
till I entered the sanctuary of God;
    then I understood their final destiny. (Ps. 73:13–17)

This encounter with God in the temple changes everything for Asaph. His situation does not change, *but his view of it does*. It is as though a window to the greater heavenly dimension was opened up before him. We see his desires undergoing a radical reorientation. No longer does he envy the godless; he is suddenly filled with horror at the notion of being in conflict with God as they are (see vv. 18–22). Moreover, he realizes that all he needs and wants in life is God. He is filled with a sense of the supreme desirability of God. His perturbed and agitated desires are stilled like a wild animal that is overcome and yields like a docile pet. His heart comes to a stunning point of tranquil rest in the simple desire for God alone. What follows are, in my opinion, the most beautiful words written in the entire Psalter:

> Yet I am always with you;
>   you hold me by my right hand.
> You guide me with your counsel,
>   and afterward you will take me into glory.
> Whom have I in heaven but you?
>   And earth has nothing I desire besides you.
> My flesh and my heart may fail,
>   but God is the strength of my heart
>   and my portion forever. . . .
>
> But as for me, it is good to be near God.
>   I have made the Sovereign LORD my refuge;
>   I will tell of all your deeds. (Ps. 73:23–26, 28)

This is true happiness. Here is proof that happiness is possible and testimony to what true happiness is. Here is a man who carried the grievous tension between his situation and the goodness of God right before the face of God. His faith strained against the strength of this tension until it burst him out of his shell, born like a bird out of its egg. And here he finds freedom—freedom from the incessant tormenting noise of unsatisfied desire. He is still and content. His desires no longer fuel his anxiety, as is so often the case, but rather they begin to fuel his relationship with God. His will is now aligned with the will of God. The concerns for subsistence, health, and protection are thus subsumed under his preoccupation with God. Being alive has no other meaning than walking with God and serving his purposes.

Happiness is the state of being in which desire finds its right orbit, a higher orbit around the true God. It is when desire detaches itself from the host of false gods that held it hostage and rises up to orbit serenely around the God who established its energy. God created humans with desire so that we can freely desire what God wants to give us. He gave us desire so that we can have the capacity to experience and enjoy the goodness of God himself.

11

THE REST OF WORSHIP

My soul finds rest in God alone;
  my salvation comes from him.
He alone is my rock and my salvation;
  he is my fortress, I will never be shaken.

Psalm 62:1–2

Soul Rest

We need rest. We need a rest for our souls that no amount of sleep or relaxation will give us. If you are like the average person, juggling work, family, church, sport, social engagements, and so forth, then you are probably exhausted. We imagine that our exhaustion will be remedied by some good sleep and a beach holiday. And perhaps, if we are physically and mentally exhausted, this will do us a lot of good. But most people are not exhausted primarily by physical and mental overactivity. This is a cause of exhaustion, but it is not the root cause. Most people don't get the rest they need because *they don't know what it is they need rest from.*

The psalms provide a picture of a kind of rest, a *vital* kind of rest that exposes a need most people don't think they have. The psalms help us to recognize this need, and they show us what it is that meets this need. It is a little like a person who has a certain food allergy but does not recognize how it affects them. Let's say they go through life feeling perpetually exhausted thinking this is just the way they are when all along a food allergy is exhausting their system. Then they meet someone who had the same condition, and they realize it is not natural at all to live like this. They are led to understand the source of their exhaustion, and, by remedying their

125

diet, they discover a vitality they never thought was possible. The psalms act as this very point of discovery. They express a vitality that is found in a soul rest that meets the deepest needs of the human soul.

Wherever happiness is expressed in the psalms, we see this rest—a deep rest of soul that defies natural explanation. It is stillness and tranquility, but it is not inactive. On the contrary, it is intensely energetic, though it appears to lack exertion. It feels like ease—even weightlessness—and yet it carries a responsibility of infinite consequence. It is not dependent on the absence of external commotion—in fact, it is often expressed in the context of severe impending military threat. It is an experience of peace, but it is untiringly militant. Any reader of the psalms will recognize the paradoxes I describe because they permeate the pages of the Psalter.

The psalms portray a process in which a restlessness of soul is overcome. The goal, soul rest, is expressed but not defined in itself. It can be defined only by the process through which it is attained. The psalms guide us as much by defining the origin as by mapping the path to the destination. Restlessness is abundantly expressed in the psalms. It feels like an agitating uncertainty that jabs the soul, continuously causing a kind of spiritual sleep-deprivation torture. It feels like the strain of a great weight upon the shoulders being cruelly and perpetually self-imposed out of a fear of what may happen if we drop it. It is the ache of unfulfilled longings nagging at the heart, like the pangs of hunger to one who is starving. It saps strength, suffocates vitality, and exhausts every emotional resource in store.

Unfortunately, most people live with these symptoms in the belief that this is life and there is no alternative. This is not life, and there *is* an alternative. In the psalms, these feelings are overcome, not by more exertion on the part of the individual but by a process of liberation wrought by God. It is remarkably simple and wonderfully possible.

Artificial Imperatives

What is it that exhausts us? Like the food allergy illustration I just used, it has to do with *intake*. We imbibe certain spiritual toxins that exhaust our systems. I am going to refer to these toxins as "artificial imperatives." They are laws imposed into our hearts that are alien and hostile to our created being. They provide some immediate satisfaction, but they inevitably poison our hearts and exhaust our wills. In the world in which the psalms were written, these artificial imperatives were represented by religious idols, of which there were many physical representations. These idols are the great nemesis of the spirituality of the psalms. They are mentioned constantly, and no discussion of the spirituality of the psalms would be complete without some reference to them. It is important, however, that we distinguish the manifestation of this toxin of idolatry from the essence of the toxin itself.

The toxin is essentially designed to inhibit human potential. It is a demonic ruse designed to incapacitate humankind and keep us in subjection. This stratagem may be packaged differently for specific appeal to each generation, but the product inside the package remains the same. For ancient Israel, the artificial imperative was packaged as the requirements of Baal, Ashtoreth, Molech, or other local Canaanite deities.

In the first century, the time of Jesus's earthly ministry, the same product was imbibed by the people but, ironically, in the form of a legalistic augmentation of the requirements of the biblical law. The packaging was made to look like biblical faith, but the contents were the same toxic mix of artificial imperatives. Jesus's charge against first-century Judaism was that it had become just another taxing religion that burdened the heart and exhausted the will. In every age, these imperatives are repackaged and imposed upon us in different ways. As in ancient times, parents, with all good intent, impose these imperatives on their children, role models exemplify them, peers alienate those who do not conform to them, and finally the entire community celebrates and promotes those who succeed in embodying them.

Let me break this down. Unless you are a remarkably spiritually advanced person, your system is probably being profoundly affected by the toxins I am talking about. You will recognize these toxins as the deep, inner compulsions that drive your life's agendas. They are those expectations that you have imbibed and accepted as law, the things you feel you *must* achieve and that you fear *not* achieving. They are the things you vow deep within yourself to do or not do with your life. These imperatives may have been culturally imposed, inherited from parents, or imposed by peers, or perhaps they are simply the result of certain experiences you have had. You may feel you must achieve certain lifestyle goals or perhaps a certain degree of success, rank, and recognition in your occupation. You may feel you must win the respect and admiration of others.

Along with this, you may inevitably harbor a fear of failure, of being a disappointment to those who expect certain things of you, of becoming disrespectable in some sense. Whatever the case, whether these examples resonate with you or not, you will inevitably have certain "I must" compulsions driving you to do what you do. It is not that we shouldn't want to succeed and achieve certain things. The problem is the feeling that we *must* achieve these things at all costs. We rarely question the validity of the authority of these inner imperatives. Most of them, in fact, have no validity at all.

The only thing we *must* do in life is the will of God. Given that we were created in accordance with God's will, this is as natural to the soul as flying is to a bird or swimming is to a fish. Far from being onerous, the doing of God's will is actually the very means by which we experience the joy of life. It is the flight path of the soul. And what's more, it is also beautifully simple. God's will is simply that we receive, reciprocate, and share his love.

There is freedom in this simplicity, but it is rarely attained. We inevitably end up striving and straining to achieve a host of elusive goals in life that God never put before us. We take these goals on ourselves, and they become the objects of the worship of our lives. The result is akin to tying a heavy burden to a bird to pull while it flies. Naturally, the joy of flight will be stifled by the endless, exhausting effort to pull a weight that has no meaning. There is no purpose to the burden other than to inhibit us.

The Easy Yoke

At the risk of mixing metaphors, imagine all those expectations you have taken on as though they were heavy rocks in a cart. We yoke ourselves to this cart and we pull it along because we are convinced that there is some value in the rocks and they are worth pulling. When we pull them a certain distance and achieve a certain goal, we feel validated and significant, when in fact the only thing we have done is waste our efforts. The rocks in the cart have no value at all. They have no purpose other than to weigh us down and keep us inhibited.

It is to those burdened by artificial imperatives, by the cart of self-imposed expectations, that Jesus comes with the invitation to find rest under his yoke. "Come to me, all you who are weary and burdened," he says, "and I will give you rest." The rest that

Jesus offers is the yoke of his agenda: that of the will of God. He continues, "Take my yoke upon you and learn from me, for I am gentle and humble in heart, and you will find rest for your souls. For my yoke is easy and my burden is light" (Matt. 11:28–30). The yoke of God's will is easy, because when we yoke ourselves to his cart, to his agenda, we don't have to pull that cart. We don't have to make that agenda happen. When we yoke ourselves to the cart of God's will, the cart pulls us. The yoke is not exhausting but empowering and liberating.

For the psalmists, the yoke of God was the Torah (the law), that is, the Word of God. When the psalmists spoke about the law, the statutes, and the decrees of God, they meant the written Word of God. For David and most of the other psalmists, this consisted of the first five books of the Bible (Genesis–Deuteronomy). The Torah was the expression of God's will for his people. The word *law* is misleading because it makes the Torah sound like a mere list of prohibitions. In fact, the law had to do primarily with the *covenant*. The covenant was God's promise to and purpose for his people. It was expressed not primarily in prohibitions but in promises about what God would do for his people. It also included large sections of narrative giving concrete historical precedents of God's covenant faithfulness to which subsequent generations could appeal.

God was showing his people a road to walk down, and the prohibitions were the barriers marking where the edge of the road was. A road is not an inhibiting thing but something that promotes efficient movement. Likewise, the psalmists did not see the Word of God as an enclosure that limited them but as a road that liberated and empowered them to live to their full potential in God. The statutes of God were invigorating to them, "reviving the soul" and "giving light to the eyes" and "joy to the heart" (Ps. 19:7–8). The Torah was a source of rest for the soul. The writer of Psalm 119, a psalm devoted mainly to celebrating the Torah, writes:

> I have chosen the way of truth;
>> I have set my heart on your laws. . . .
> I run in the path of your commands,
>> for you have set my heart free. (vv. 30, 32)

It is important, when we read references to the Torah in the psalms, that we take into view a deeper referent than simply words on a page. The Word of God is the expression of God himself, and to receive it into the heart is to receive God. In a sense, the written Word is the outward linguistic representation of the personal Word, which we ultimately see incarnate in Jesus Christ. It is this Word that is deposited into our hearts by the Holy Spirit. Jeremiah speaks of the law being written on the hearts of the people (Jer. 31), and Ezekiel speaks of God placing his Spirit within them (Ezek. 36).

David and the writers of the psalms experienced this, as did all those who were used by God to create the canon of Scripture. When they received the Word, they were clearly receiving more than abstract ideas. As they imbibed the Word, they were being filled with the Spirit, and so the Word became "more precious than gold" and "sweeter than honey" (Ps. 19:10). As they obeyed the Torah and lived by the Spirit, they experienced the essence of worship. It was not an onerous religious yoke. It was a yoke that drew them along with God, and it was a delightful and exhilarating life.

Transferral

Throughout the psalms, a profound process of transferral takes place. One yoke is replaced with another. The exodus experience is enacted over and over again. The yoke of slavery is replaced by the yoke of God. This process is the essence of what we call worship, and it is essential that we allow the psalms to define worship in accordance with this process. It is important to understand worship on a continuum. Worship is a motion away from autonomy and toward God. It is an act of renunciation and reappropriation. We renounce our autonomy, we give up the right to set the goals for our lives, and we come under the authority of God.

Of course, autonomy does not really exist for human beings. If we are not ruled by God, we create an authority vacuum over our lives that is inevitably filled with a tangled web of competing claims over our hearts. This state of affairs was much more clearly evident in the world of the psalms than in our time. Either the people were given over to God or they were given over to idols. Idols represented the various claimants to supremacy over the heart.

The act of giving oneself over to God was symbolized in the offerings of sacrifices that many psalms were originally intended to accompany. The offerings represented the individuals who presented the offerings. An offering was a gesture of entrusting oneself to God. Expressions of *trust* abound in the psalms, and these are key indicators of the momentum of worship taking place in the psalms. To worship is not just to offer compliments to God but to offer *oneself* to God, not as a gift but as something that always rightfully belonged to him (cf. Rom. 12:1). Worship is therefore giving God what is due to him, not just our service and our obedience but our very selves. We can obey and serve God to a self-gratifying extent without ever trusting in him. The entrusting of oneself to God is the essence of worship.

Invulnerability

A common metaphor used in the psalms to portray the experience of trust is that of finding refuge in a fortress. Such a metaphor was close to the hearts of a people who lived in constant vulnerability to military invasion and banditry. It highlights the fact that unrest has a lot to do with the fears associated with vulnerability. We may not fear military threats, but any person alienated from God will inevitably face a daunting vulnerability and will live in the same unrest. Let's face it, there is a lot that can go wrong in life, and your imagination will no doubt have represented every possible scenario to you. The fear associated with vulnerability is the dread of being overpowered, of losing control. This for any person is the root of all fear.

One of the most remarkable experiences portrayed in the psalms is the experience of invulnerability. This is where the metaphor of refuge and fortress is used. "God is my fortress," declares the psalmist, "therefore we will not fear" (Ps. 46). It is said again and again in a number of ways. To penetrate the nature of this experience, however, we need to go deeper than the obvious. The psalmists did not feel invulnerable because they believed nothing bad would ever happen to them. Their lack of fear was the result of an act of renunciation. Trusting God is much more than trusting God *for something*. It is the will to be overpowered by God, to entrust one's life to God and thereby renounce the right to set the agendas for one's own life.

By allowing themselves to be overpowered by God, the psalmists put themselves into a bigger picture. They stepped up into the purpose of God, which cannot be thwarted. So whatever happened, even if they suffered loss for a time, they did not feel vulnerable or afraid because they recognized that they were in God's purpose and God was sovereign over their circumstances. The safest place in the world is in the will of God. As long as they walked in his "paths of righteousness," they remained undaunted. When they walked through "the valley of the shadow of death," as they often did, they were comforted by the "rod and staff" of God's authority over them, as Psalm 23 famously portrays. They were not in charge, and therefore they weren't vulnerable. They were encased in God's purpose, and they knew that was a sure thing.

Rest comes from letting ourselves be overpowered by God. He has an absolute claim on our lives, and as long as we deny that claim, we are in conflict, and conflict is unrest. There is only one way to end the conflict: surrender.

Imagine your life as a walled city whose ramparts, towers, and palaces represent your agendas and achievements. Defending this city is a daunting task because it is not as strong as it seems. In fact, it is very brittle. There is no rest in the city. Imagine then that God draws up to the city. He comes to stake his claim upon you—not as a tyrant coming to plunder but as a father coming to win back a son or a daughter. What you must do is simply walk out of the city and surrender it to him. Give it all to him. Allow God to overpower you. This is worship. As you allow God to overpower you, God's authority overshadows you, and there is no fear in the shadow of God's authority. There is only peace and rest.

> He who dwells in the shelter of the Most High
>   will rest in the shadow of the Almighty.
> I will say of the Lord, "He is my refuge and my
>   fortress,
>   my God, in whom I trust." (Ps. 91:1–2)

12

THE POWER OF DEBT

> How can I repay the LORD
>   for all his goodness to me?
> I will lift up the cup of salvation
>   and call on the name of the LORD.
>
>   Psalm 116:12–13

Positive Debt

You need more debt. Debt empowers, and the more in debt you are, the more empowered you will be. I am not talking here about financial debt, though this association helps to illustrate how negative a concept debt has become in our minds. Intuitively, debt is associated with *weakness*. The more indebted we are to someone, the weaker we feel. The association of debt with weakness applies logically within a system where the values of autonomy, independence, and competitiveness reign supreme. In a competitive system, as has characterized the human world since the fall of man, debt signals dependence and subjugation—hardly empowering ideas in most people's minds. In the psalms, however, we see another system at work, and it is here that the remarkable connection between debt and empowerment is expressed.

Indebtedness creates a strong bond between two persons that remains as long as the debt remains. The debtor is bound to the one he is in debt to, and the greater the debt, the greater the bond. For most people, the idea of being bound to another person is intensely negative, and this is not surprising. In most cases in the world today, a debt empowers the giver rather than the receiver: I do something for you or give you something, and I thereby gain power over you and the right to extract certain forms of obeisance from you. This whole system is the negative inversion of a system of debt that God created to strengthen relationships. This negative inversion is so firmly established in the world that we may struggle to wrest the idea of indebtedness from these negative associations. But these negative associations rob us of one of the most important relational interchanges between humans and God demonstrated in the psalms.

It goes without saying that we are indebted to God. We start life with a debt to God because he is the one who gave us life. Everything that God does for us throughout our lives, every act of providence, kindness, blessing, even discipline, adds to the debt we owe to God. The gift of salvation in the sacrifice of Jesus Christ is so unimaginably great that it increases the debt beyond what our minds can grasp.

There are things that God does for you every day that you don't notice. He protects you, guides you, teaches you, and helps you. So much divine activity surrounds your life that to describe what takes place in one minute would take an entire lifetime. Infinite love and goodness are at work in you and over you constantly. God "will neither slumber nor sleep," says the psalmist. "The LORD will watch over your coming and going both now and forevermore" (Ps. 121: 4, 8). "He will command his angels concerning you," says the writer of Psalm 91, "to guard you in all your ways; they will lift you up in their hands, so that you will not strike your foot against a stone" (vv. 11–12). The descriptions of the love and goodness of God in the psalms go on and on. They come from an awareness of debt that is opened up by a willingness to be overpowered by God.

The Implications of Gratitude

It is easy to say thank you to God, but it is something else again to arrive at a genuine experience of gratitude. The psalms abound with expressions of genuine gratitude, and the psalmists were not just being polite. The thanksgiving psalms are not like the thank-you card we send because it is the socially acceptable thing to do. Thanksgiving is not a religious obligation that is done so as not to offend God. The thanksgiving we see throughout the Psalter is the result of a willingness to acknowledge indebtedness to God that is far from intuitive. It is the renunciation of all personal entitlement in view of the overwhelming debt we owe to God.

If I asked if you were grateful to God, you would probably say yes just because it would seem offensive to say otherwise. But do you really *feel* grateful? Perhaps you do to some extent because you can bring to mind recent blessings of God in your life. Or perhaps you feel nothing. Either way, your response will be disproportionate to what God has done and is doing for you. The reason we feel so little in proportion to the debt we owe to God is that we tend to hold back. We hold back because real gratitude arises from an acknowledgment of indebtedness that inevitably strips away our sense of independence. Let me give you an example of this from a human relationship.

I cowrite and coproduce music with a very close friend who is, in my mind, something of a musical genius. He has had a huge effect on the way I write and play music. He is easily the biggest musical influence in my life. His breadth of musical expertise and out-of-the-box creativity have given our psalms project band, Sons of Korah, its unique sound. With some hesitation, I openly confess that it has been difficult for me to acknowledge the extent of my indebtedness to this man. I like to think I am an independent source of unlimited musical creativity. I don't like feeling dependent upon someone else, so I resist that feeling of indebtedness and have in the past too often failed to acknowledge this debt fully. For some reason, I have felt disempowered by indebtedness, so I have tried to pump up the value of my own contribution to eclipse his. I was so focused on wanting him to recognize the debt he owed to me that I failed to recognize the debt I owed to him. He would be quick to reciprocate the sense of indebtedness, I'm sure much more easily than I do. But can you see from this example how being truly grateful is a far deeper process than the shallow offer of polite thanks? If we hold back from acknowledging debt like this with other people, how much more with God, to whom we owe infinite debt?

The Sacrifice of Thanksgiving

There is always a sacrifice in gratitude. This is expressed in the apparent close connection between the thanksgiving psalms and the sacrifices of thanksgiving. Thanksgiving was an important formalized aspect of the corporate worship of Old Testament Israel. Throughout the biblical narratives, we see people responding to God's goodness by offering sacrifices in the temple. In many lament psalms, the psalmists make vows to God to the effect that if he were to save them, they would declare his praise *before the assembly of God's people.* Corresponding to this, then, we find in many thanksgiving psalms the conscious sense of *fulfilling a vow* previously made to God in this kind of circumstance. The vow is fulfilled as the psalmist declares his testimony publicly, and part of this public declaration is the offering of the prescribed sacrifice of thanksgiving. Here is an example:

> Set me free from my prison,
>   that I may praise your name.
> Then the righteous will gather about me
>   because of your goodness to me. (Ps. 142:7)

I will fulfill my vows to the LORD
  in the presence of all his people.

Precious in the sight of the LORD
  is the death of his saints.
O LORD, truly I am your servant;
  I am your servant, the son of your maidservant;
  you have freed me from my chains.

I will sacrifice a thank offering to you
  and call on the name of the LORD.
I will fulfill my vows to the LORD
  in the presence of all his people,
in the courts of the house of the LORD—
  in your midst, O Jerusalem.

Praise the LORD. (Ps. 116:14–19)

The offerings of thanks presented to God on these occasions were public declarations of indebtedness to God. The people celebrated God's faithfulness, but the offerings themselves signified the implications of realizing one's indebtedness to God. The sacrifice represented the giving of oneself to God. It was an act of surrender invoked by the disarming experience of the goodness and faithfulness of God. In the light of God's manifest goodness, any excuse there may have been not to trust God was extinguished. The offerings used to express gratitude (Lev. 3 and 7), in other words, signified the people's willingness to be so completely in God's debt as to relinquish any sense of independence and autonomy. The moment of gratitude was the supreme reality check. When God overpowers our circumstances, he overpowers us.

To be truly grateful, to allow ourselves to feel indebted to any other person and most of all to God, we have to be willing to give up the masquerade of independence. This is no easy matter because it grates against one of our deepest inclinations. Self-dependence is the central pillar of the human endeavor for autonomy and independence, an endeavor that has driven the human heart since our first ancestors broke away from God in a desire to be gods unto themselves. The rest is history. Thousands of years of mutual human betrayal have made a virtue of self-dependence. Self-dependence, however, far from being a valuable attribute, is a complete delusion. You and I are nothing without God (and we are not much without the people God has put around us). We are dependent on God as much as branches are dependent on a tree. Moreover, God created human beings to be mutually dependent. That we spurn the latter is a natural result of having denied the former.

If it is so counterintuitive for us to acknowledge our relative dependence on other people, how much more difficult it must be to acknowledge our absolute dependence on God. Throughout the narratives of the history of Israel, it is remarkable how stubborn the people were in their refusal to trust God. If they did trust God, it was often a last resort. The experience should be familiar to all of us who begin by trying to work things out on our own and turn to God only when we find we can't do something ourselves. Why do we do this? Why not begin with God? We don't know what potential there is in us until our lives are inhabited by God.

Dependence is not a weakness; it is a *strength*. The fact that we were created to be dependent on God signifies the exalted position we were created to occupy in the universal hierarchy. We were created to be God's children and vessels of his glory and power. With God, we are the crown of creation for whom nothing is impossible. Without God, we are nothing. The choice we must make to reconnect with our purpose and potential is the choice to allow ourselves to be overpowered by God. We must be willing to face the reality that we are indebted to God for all that we are and be prepared to be indebted to God for everything we will be and do in life. We must relinquish any right to receive ultimate credit for anything. "Not to us, O LORD," says the psalmist, and then he repeats himself to make it emphatic: "not to us but to your name be the glory, because of your love and faithfulness" (Ps. 115:1). This leads him to articulate the implied imperative:

> O Israel, trust in the LORD!
> He is their help and their shield.
> O house of Aaron, trust in the LORD!
> He is their help and their shield.
> You who fear the LORD, trust in the LORD!
> He is their help and their shield. (Ps. 115:9–11 ESV)

The acknowledgment of indebtedness leads to the compulsion to trust. The sacrifice of independence inherent in acts of true gratitude liberates the soul to cleave to God again. This is the sequence that takes place in the heart, and it is articulated in many of the psalms. The acknowledgment of what God has done in the past is the spring that propels the heart to trust God. Thanksgiving and praise are preliminary steps toward the faith and confidence we see expressed in the many "therefore I will not be afraid" statements in the psalms. The psalmist declares what God has done in detail, and from this arises the unshakable confidence that God will do it again.

> I love the LORD, for he heard my voice;
> he heard my cry for mercy.
> Because he turned his ear to me,
> I will call on him as long as I live.

The cords of death entangled me,
    the anguish of the grave came upon me;
    I was overcome by trouble and sorrow.
Then I called on the name of the LORD:
    "O LORD, save me!"

The LORD is gracious and righteous;
    our God is full of compassion.
The LORD protects the simplehearted;
    when I was in great need, he saved me.

Be at rest once more, O my soul,
    for the LORD has been good to you. (Ps. 116:1–7)

The Power of Celebration

Gratitude empowers. This is what we learn from the testimonial thanksgiving psalms, like Psalm 116 quoted above. The psalmists are not just saying a polite thank you; they are celebrating the salvation and providence of God and, by implication, their debt to God. When they did this, they opened their hearts to be overpowered by God, and this is how they gained the remarkable confidence in the face of adversity that characterizes the pages of the Psalter. As the people celebrated the past acts of God, they transformed their perception of the present. Note the process in Psalm 77:

I cried out to God for help;
    I cried out to God to hear me.
When I was in distress, I sought the Lord;
    at night I stretched out untiring hands
    and my soul refused to be comforted. . . .

"Will the Lord reject forever?
    Will he never show his favor again?

144

Has his unfailing love vanished forever?
　　Has his promise failed for all time?
Has God forgotten to be merciful?
　　Has he in anger withheld his compassion?"

Then I thought, "To this I will appeal:
　　the years of the right hand of the Most High."
I will remember the deeds of the LORD;
　　yes, I will remember your miracles of long ago.
I will meditate on all your works
　　and consider all your mighty deeds.

Your ways, O God, are holy.
　　What god is so great as our God?
You are the God who performs miracles;
　　you display your power among the peoples.
With your mighty arm you redeemed your people,
　　the descendants of Jacob and Joseph. (vv. 1–2,
　　　7–15)

Here we see the remembrance and celebration of past acts of God lifting the psalmist to an attitude of triumph before any change in his outward circumstances. He is indomitable. The celebration of God's past acts has built his faith and empowered his spirit. He is not whipping himself up into an emotionally positive attitude. This is not just spiritual self-motivation. The psalmist is breaking out of his self-dependence. He is allowing himself to believe that he is powerless without God and thereby allowing himself to be overpowered by God. This is an act of worship and surrender.

The connection between celebration and faith is so important for the building of trust that the practices of commemoration and celebration were built into the Israelite calendar from the beginning. God knew that his people needed to maintain their sense of indebtedness to him. They needed to be reminded continually of how they came to be where they were and who it was that brought them there.

For every major historical event in the history of Israel, there was an annual celebration during which the acts of God were remembered and even reenacted. The Passover Feast and the Feast of Unleavened Bread were celebrations of God's deliverance of the Israelites from Egypt. The Feast of Tabernacles was a reminder to the Israelites of God's provision during the forty years in the desert under Moses. The Feast of Purim was celebrated to remind the Jewish people of God's deliverance from what would otherwise have been genocide during the time of Esther. The Jews added to this the Feast of Hanukkah, which celebrated the victories of the Maccabees and the rededication of the temple in 165 BC. The purpose of these festivals was to build *debt*. The greater the sense of debt we have, the less independent we feel. The remembrance of the acts of God therefore empowered the people inasmuch as it compelled them to recognize their dependence on God.

> "If the Lord had not been on our side . . ."
> (Israel should repeat this.)
> "If the Lord had not been on our side when people
>   attacked us,
>   then they would have swallowed us alive
>   when their anger exploded against us.
>   Then the floodwaters would have swept us away.
>   An overflowing stream would have washed us
>   away.
>   Then raging water would have washed us away."
>
> Thank the LORD, who did not let them sink their
>   teeth into us.
> We escaped like a bird caught in a hunter's trap.
>   The trap was broken, and we escaped.

146

Our help is in the name of the LORD, the maker of
heaven and earth. (Ps. 124 GW)

Facing Backward

We can't see the future, but we can see the past. God calls us
to walk forward facing backward. Our confidence in what
God will do for us comes from our ability to celebrate what
God *has done*. If you want to gain momentum to spearhead
the future, get your run-up from the past. Celebrate what
God has done for you, not in general but specifically, as the
psalmists did. The psalms also teach us that we don't just
have our own past to draw on. There is a corporate past
that belongs to us by virtue of our inclusion in the family of
God. What God does for one person is an indication of his
willingness to bless everyone. We should celebrate, therefore,
the breakthroughs of others. God speaks through what he
does, and what he does in the life of one is always a message to all.

The biblical narratives are not just inspiring stories of
things God did long ago. They are meant to be celebrated
and appealed to as precedents for what is available to us. As we
celebrate the foundational acts of God recorded in Scripture,
we build a heart connection to what is indeed the foundation of faith. Once this heart connection is established, these
events can begin to shape our expectations for the future.
The act of celebration therefore moves beyond the objective
acknowledgment of historical data. By celebrating an act of
God, we appropriate the facts personally and build a sense
of personal indebtedness to God. As the debt deepens, our
self-conceit erodes. As our pretense to independence is broken
down, we are enabled to rest more and more in our dependence on God. Dependence, in turn, breaks down our sense

147

of autonomy, allowing us to be overpowered and therefore empowered by God.

Empowering Debt

The psalms show us how cultivating a deep sense of indebtedness to God positions us to receive abundantly from God. Indebtedness erodes the deception of independence that defrauds us of untold riches of life in God. By acknowledging the pervasive role God constantly performs in our lives, we begin to acclimate to the idea that we are indeed completely dependent on him. This sense of dependence is what makes us receptive to him. God is always willing to give, but we are not always willing to receive from him simply because we tend to prefer sources we can control. Once we build this sense of dependence, however, we become much more open to the possibilities God has for us. His life can again begin to flow through us to activate our full potential. This is how debt empowers. It empowers us because it binds us to the one who is the source of the power we need to live to our full potential.

Debt compounds very quickly. The more we receive from God, the more indebted we become to him, and the more dependent we become. The more dependent we become, the more we are compelled to receive from him, and so the debt grows. I am conscious of how counterintuitive this is. There is so much within us that cries, "Danger!" Dependence is indeed a dangerous thing when it involves an abdication of productivity or when there is reason to mistrust the motives of the giver. To become willingly dependent on God, however, is simply to face reality, for in actual fact we *are* completely dependent on God. Moreover, God does not give in a way that makes our capacities for productivity redundant. God pours his Spirit into us to empower those capacities for kingdom productivity. It is only by God's power that we can achieve the things he wants us to achieve in this life. There is no reason to doubt God's intentions in this respect. He loves us and seeks the best for us always.

The practice of thanksgiving is therefore much more important than we might think. It is not, as I said, just a matter of being polite. The psalmists sought not only to express gratitude but also to cultivate gratitude. As they built their sense of indebtedness to God, they were positioned to receive in greater measure from God. Debt binds us to the one in whose debt we remain. Whether this is a good or bad thing depends on whom we are bound to. If it is God, then there can be no bond more life-giving and empowering.

Let yourself be deeply in God's debt. Spend time reflecting on what God has done for you and what he continues to do for you. Say it out loud, write it down, sing about it, and tell others. This is what the psalmists exhort us to do in response to God's goodness, and they tell us this because it is empowering to do so.

> Give thanks to the Lord.
> Call on him.
> Make known among the nations what he has done.
> Sing to him.
> Make music to praise him.
> Meditate on all the miracles he has performed.
> Brag about his holy name.
> Let the hearts of those who seek the Lord rejoice.
> Search for the Lord and his strength.
> Always seek his presence.
> Remember the miracles he performed,
>> the amazing things he did, and the judgments he
>> pronounced. (Ps. 105:1–5 GW)

149

13

JOY IS LOVE

Satisfy us in the morning with your unfailing love,
that we may sing for joy and be glad all our days.

Psalm 90:14

Love Is Joy

The greatest moments of joy in life tend to be connected with an experience of love. Remember when you experienced the first influx of joy in being loved by someone in a romantic relationship? That initial moment in a relationship is unique, and it is a taste of something that ignites the soul like nothing else.

There is something indescribably invigorating about knowing that someone whom we admire really loves us. Of all the people that person could choose, he or she is choosing us. It is intensely affirming, and there seems to be no greater need in the human soul than for personal affirmation. By personal affirmation, I mean the affirmation, not of anything objective such as achievements or appearance, but of our very *self*. Affirmation for achievements and appearance can provide a great measure of satisfaction, but it is far shallower than the affirmation of being loved for who we really are. We will never be content if we are affirmed only for what we have or do. We long to be loved as a *subject*, not as an *object*. We are not the sum of our perceptible attributes, and deep down we know that when a person loves those attributes, they are not really loving us.

The the problem is, no human being can have an exhaustive knowledge of who we really are. And since others' perceptions do not penetrate into our true self, neither does their love. Only the knowledge of God penetrates into the fullness of who and what we are. Only the love of God can permeate the depths of our being and affirm all that we are. The love of God is the foundation of our sense of identity and personal significance. There is no emptiness greater than when this love is absent. Conversely, there is no greater joy for the human soul than the joy of this love. And since this love is infinite and its subject inexhaustibly wonderful, it never fades in its impact.

Joy Is Relational

The most commonly celebrated attribute of God in the psalms is the *love* of God. In Psalm 136 alone, the line "his love endures forever" is repeated twenty-six times. A quick concordance search will show that, compared to any other attribute mentioned in the psalms, the love of God is mentioned more than everything else many times over. Add to this all the expressions of love, such as mercy, compassion, grace, favor, etc., and you will quickly see where the foundation of the joy of the Psalter lies.

Hand in hand with this attribute is the all-encompassing knowledge of God. The Hebrew notion of being "known" carries a deep relational sense. The same word is used to describe the sexual union of a man and woman in other biblical texts. In Psalm 139, the psalmist celebrates this attribute: "O Lord, you have searched me and you know me" (v. 1). Though the penetrating knowledge of God is a matter of discomfort for those who are in conflict with God, for this psalmist, it is "precious" because it implies the pervasive scope of God's love for him.

154

Wherever there is an expression of joy in the psalms, there is a celebration of God's love. The connection is profoundly instructive, particularly against the backdrop of a world trying to find joy in objects, objectives, and the objectification of people. The psalms teach us that joy is *relational*. It is not the result of possessing things or achieving certain goals. It is the result of a connection between subjects, primarily our connection with the person of God. It arises when desire is liberated to find its goal in God. When our desires lock onto God, we find that his desires have previously locked onto us. As we pursue God, we come to realize that he first pursued us. There is no greater affirmation than to be the object of the desire of God. To be loved with such persistence and sacrifice by the God who created the universe is the greatest truth our minds can lay hold of.

Out of Abstraction

For too many Christians, however, the love of God is an abstract fact that has little impact on their conscious experience. The very nature of love dictates that love must always be a matter of real experience. God's love remains a fact whatever we feel at any given time, but it must never remain *just* an abstract fact to us. God wants us to *feel* loved. As I have said, the psalms highlight the fact that feelings are important. They are important because God is interested in relationship, and relationship involves the full expression and validation of feelings. If we don't feel loved by God, then there is a problem. We should never be content with this state of affairs.

This brings us back to where we started in this book. If God seems remote and abstract to you, it may be that you are living in the protective shell described in chapter 3. Maybe you once encountered the love of God in a real way, but then the experience receded. If that is the case, it is likely that your shell grew back, as they have a habit of doing. The psalms portray a journey in which individuals are brought into a real experience of God's love often through terrible adversities that have the effect of cracking and breaking open their shells. This is the "sowing in tears" that, according to Psalm 126, leads to the "reaping with joy."

This does not mean that we have to go through hardship to be broken open and exposed again to the love of God. It does mean, though, that we should bemoan our state before God. If we are alienated from God, we should allow ourselves to feel this emptiness and let it drive us to seek God earnestly, as many psalmists do. If emptiness and alienation is your present reality then allow yourself to face that reality and take it to God so that he can lead you out. God wants you to know his love, not just know *about* it. The psalms show us a pathway to a real encounter with God and the way to walk along that pathway with him.

14

THE PRAISE
OF ENJOYMENT

I will praise you, O LORD, with all my heart;
  I will tell of all your wonders.
I will be glad and rejoice in you;
  I will sing praise to your name, O Most High.

Psalm 9:1–2

To Enjoy God

"What is the chief end of man?" This is the first question posed by one of the greatest Protestant catechisms, the Westminster Shorter Catechism. It is an appropriate way to begin a summary statement of Christian belief because there is no more important, practical question we could ask about our lives. It is the same question as, "What is the meaning of life?" The answer is a wonderful statement not only about our purpose but also about the nature of God: "The chief end of man is to glorify God and enjoy him forever." As I will demonstrate here, glorifying and enjoying are closely related, and the psalms demonstrate this connection better than any other part of Scripture.

We glorify God as we enjoy God, and we enjoy God as we glorify him. It is a wonderful statement about the loving, parental nature of God that he should seek our *enjoyment* rather than just our obedience. The psalms reveal a deeply relational interchange between people and God that includes at its highest point the enjoyment of God. The idea of enjoyment as a human experience is much more familiar to most of us than the more elusive concept of glorifying. So given the close connection between the two ideas, the former is a good place to begin to understand the latter.

The most powerful statement of someone's worth to us is our desire to enjoy them for who they are. There is no deeper expression of my love for my wife than for me to genuinely enjoy her companionship. This is what a personal relationship is all about. To love someone is to enjoy them, not as an object but as a subject in all of their uniqueness. When we enjoy another person, we are affirming and celebrating who that person is; we are declaring something about that person's worth to us.

I have found this to be important with my children too. It is so easy to focus just on how exhausting children can be. I have found, though, that one of the most important things I can do for my children is not just to feed, clothe, and transport them around but to *enjoy* them. When I enjoy my children, I am struck by how affirming this is for them. It affirms them in a way that no words of affirmation can get close to doing. Enjoyment of another person in the genuinely relational sense is, in other words, the highest praise one can offer to affirm the worth of that person.

What applies to our various human relationships applies in a fundamental sense to our relationship with God. He does not need to be affirmed for his sake, but he wants to be *enjoyed*. In fact, this is what he wants more than anything else. There is no gesture of praise to God greater than genuine enjoyment of God. And there is no statement of divine worthiness more compelling to other people than for them to see us enjoying God.

If it is true that God wants us to enjoy him—and the overwhelming evidence of Scripture affirms that it is—then this underlines a point I have been emphasizing right from the start of this book. It becomes the ultimate rationale behind my insistence that we should never be content with an abstract faith. Enjoyment is a real experience. We cannot enjoy someone if we only know *about* that person. Objective knowledge is not enough; we need subjective knowledge. To enjoy someone, we need to meet and connect with him or her personally.

It is not enough for us to know that God forgives us and is favorably disposed toward us. We cannot fulfill the purpose of our existence from this standpoint. To enjoy God requires a real relational connection with a real God and a real experience of his love for us. This is why God pours his Spirit into our hearts: so that we can know him from a proximity closer than any human relationship. This brings us right up to the high point of the psalms. At the highest point of the spiritual journey portrayed by the Psalter, we find people enjoying God. In their enjoyment of God, they become vessels of praise to God. This deeper sense of praise is precisely what it means to "glorify." We can praise God in a shallower sense with words alone, but we can only glorify God by *enjoying* him.

Vessels of Praise

Praise is therefore not primarily a verbal act. It is expressed verbally, but it is primarily a state of being. In many praise psalms, the psalmist calls on animals and even inanimate objects such as trees, mountains, and oceans to praise the Lord. This is not just poetic froth. In Psalm 19, David asserts directly that even inanimate creation can indeed declare the glory of God. Though he speaks poetically about their voice and their speech, what they say is in fact far beyond what any amount of rhetoric could express. They give testimony to God's greatness by *what they are*, by their very *being*. This is the act of praise in its foundational sense. It is not primarily verbal. The verbal act is an expression of a state of being, a state of connection with and enjoyment of God.

Praise the LORD from the earth,
>you great sea creatures and all ocean depths,
lightning and hail, snow and clouds,
>stormy winds that do his bidding,
you mountains and all hills,
>fruit trees and all cedars. (Ps. 148:7–9)

Praise in this sense permeates the psalms whatever the mood. Even in the darkest laments there is praise, if only in the sense that the psalmist persists in seeking God through his grief. He is declaring much about God simply by this pursuit. He declares the desirability of God as he bemoans his alienation from God. He declares the compassion of God in his belief that God will hear him. He declares the faithfulness of God in his appeals to the promises of God. Throughout the psalms in different ways, the disposition of praise is abundantly expressed in an indirect sense even where there is no direct verbal praise.

Some of the most powerful verbal expressions of praise, however, are those made in the context of grief. Here the psalmists commend themselves to God and use praise to urge themselves on in their pursuit of God. And if these verbal acts of praise do indeed prove to be effective, it is only because their lives are already expressing praise by the very pursuit itself.

Creation may declare the glory of God, but there are only a certain amount of things the inanimate creation and even the animal world can declare about God. They are a testimony to God's power, wisdom, knowledge, sovereignty, and so forth. But they cannot express what is upheld in the psalms and the rest of Scripture as the crowning attribute of God, namely, his *love*. Other parts of creation can act as symbols of love in that they testify to what God has provided for us, but they do not, in themselves, express much more about the love of God.

To declare this attribute, one must embody it. To declare God's love, one must love and be loved by God. This is possible only for people. God affirms his creation as good, but humans were created to be more than good: We were created to be objects of *love*. We are God's children, and there is nothing like a child to make manifest the love of a parent. Even when we cease to be good, we remain loved. In fact, by virtue of having ceased to be naturally good, we are able to manifest the greatest expression of the love of God, his *grace*. Adam before the fall could not commend the grace of God. Only we who have ceased to be good can do that. This does not mean, of course, that rebellion glorifies God, for it is only in our response of faith to the grace of God that these attributes become manifest. Until we turn from sin and respond to God in faith, our lives only disparage his love and grace.

We declare the wonders of the nature of God by *enjoying God*. The preeminence given to the enjoyment of God in the Psalms expresses the unique relational nature of biblical spirituality. This priority casts biblical spirituality far away from being a mere religion to observe. It shows that having a relationship with God is not meant to be an onerous task but something desirable, not as a means to another end but desirable in itself. That God wants, above all, to be enjoyed bespeaks the beautiful relational simplicity of the biblical faith. God just wants us to enjoy ourselves in him and perpetuate that joy by spreading it to others. This is an alternate expression of the greatest commandment. God simply wants us to love him, to love being with him, to delight in his presence, and to enjoy his goodness and love. This is how the glory of God is manifest in us. That is the basic element of praise.

Of course, even those who reject God will finally have to recognize the sovereignty and justice of God, but God most wants to be represented as *loving* and *gracious*. These are relational attributes that, if they are not enjoyed in relationship with God, are inevitably disparaged. The best thing we can do, then, and it is marvelously simple, is to enjoy God. If we enjoy him, we become vessels of his glory before anything is said.

15

THE FLIGHT OF JOY

Praise the LORD.

Praise God in his sanctuary;
   praise him in his mighty heavens.
Praise him for his acts of power;
   praise him for his surpassing greatness.
Praise him with the sounding of the trumpet,
   praise him with the harp and lyre,
praise him with tambourine and dancing,
   praise him with the strings and flute,
praise him with the clash of cymbals,
   praise him with resounding cymbals.

Let everything that has breath praise the LORD.

Praise the LORD.

Psalm 150

Words of Praise

Praise is not primarily verbal, it is a state of being. But verbal praise is a necessary extension of our enjoyment of God. The ability to communicate is closely associated with our unique nature as God's image bearers. God is a relational God who speaks things into being and desires to communicate with his people. Likewise, we are relational creatures with the capacity to communicate. Verbal expression is a key aspect of being human. It is also a natural outlet for feeling. Verbalizing a feeling is actually a necessary part of allowing ourselves to *feel* a feeling.

The feeling that flows from enjoyment is joy. Throughout the psalms, joy is expressed in the verbal effusion of rejoicing. The oft-repeated imperative to *rejoice* in the psalms is not meant to be a statement of religious obligation. It is an invitation to maximize enjoyment by letting the flow of joy intensify through outward expression. If the outflow of joy is inhibited, it clots like blood and stops flowing. Joy must be expressed in order to be perpetuated. Verbal praise, therefore, is an act of enjoyment, that is, an act by which we seek to perpetuate joy.

Another thing about verbal expression is that we need someone to whom we can express ourselves. This again is a

natural aspect of our humanness. We are community creatures, and we are made to live relationally. Hence, joy must
be *shared* in order to be fully experienced. If we don't share
our enjoyment, we impede the momentum of our enjoyment.
We all know the feeling, when something marvellous happens
to us, of needing to tell someone. It seems that the deepest
emotions of the heart demand a communal expression to
achieve expressive satisfaction. These deep, emotional experiences seem to access the deepest places of our souls where our
sense of commonality and kinship with others lies. It is the
case with grief, and it is the case with joy. If it isn't shared,
it feels like it is being suppressed.

The Synergy of Corporate Praise

The act of praise is not simply to provide God with a list of
compliments, as though he needs to be encouraged about
his self-image. It is not like the flattery we give to a powerful
person in order to win their favor. God doesn't need to be
told how great he is. What he wants, and it is worth saying
again, is for us to *enjoy* him. The act of praise, as we see it
abundantly expressed in the jubilant praise psalms, is essentially an act of enjoyment. We perpetuate joy by expressing
joy, and we express joy through praise.

To praise God, we need other people. Praise is essentially a
communal activity. Celebration is not really celebration when
we are on our own. There is a certain synergy in communal
enjoyment. Joy seems to gain in intensity when it is taken
up and expressed by more people. We experience this in any
activity in which we find enjoyment. If we gather with other
people who have the same passion for an activity, we find our
own enjoyment greatly expanded. If we combine a number
of burning sticks, we get a bonfire that increases the energy

of the fire in each individual stick. If we want our joy to burn brighter, the key is to share it with others.

It is interesting to note in the psalms of praise how often the psalmists call other people to praise the Lord with them. When the psalmist declares his intention to praise God, it is often followed by the words "in the great assembly" or "in the congregation." And even where this is not explicitly stated, it is always implicit. The assumption in the psalms is that we need other people to praise God *to*. The primary audience of the act of praise is not God but other people. Praise, therefore, is the act of enjoying God *with other people*.

This is a wonderful way to understand the act of praise because it wrenches it away from an unfortunate religious association. At times, I feel that the imperative to praise God is taken as though it were a solemn duty we must fulfill in order to have done the right thing by God. This is where we get all the arguments about the right way to do it, as though praise involves fulfilling an onerous religious obligation. To approach God like this is to treat him like the gods of ancient times who had to be appeased by the fulfillment of specific lists of requirements.

We should not, by the way, conceive the sacrificial system of the Old Testament in this way. The reason why it was so important to approach God with exactly the right sacrifices and in exactly the prescribed way was because the sacrificial system was three-dimensional theology. To change an element of the sacrificial ceremony was to mess with the theology being conveyed symbolically through that ceremony. God was not telling us through the sacrificial system that we can celebrate at his party only if we follow a meticulously complex system of table manners.

When David danced before God and the ark as it was being brought up to the temple (2 Sam. 6:14), he was not following a prescribed set of dance steps that would alone please God. He was spontaneously expressing his joy. He did, however, have to ensure that the ark was carried by the prescribed Levite representatives. There were, in other words, important theological considerations that needed to be respected, but within these boundaries, there was room to celebrate freely and spontaneously.

The Bible gives us boundaries for all aspects of life that are designed not to impede our enjoyment of life and of God but to *enlarge* it. Everything is for our good, and the highest good is to glorify God and enjoy him forever. Once we understand the principles that give us these boundaries, we should not think that there is a "right way" to praise God. Within these boundaries, we should simply praise God in the most enjoyable way possible.

Beyond Words

Joy needs more than words for its expression. The jubilant praise psalms encourage us to go beyond verbal expressions to express our joy. The psalms themselves were never meant to be verbal expressions *alone*. They were written as *songs* to be sung and to be accompanied by musical instruments. We are not just exhorted to praise God in the psalms; we are exhorted again and again to *sing* praise to God, and we are encouraged to use instruments to amplify the expression of our emotions. As Victor Hugo said, "Music expresses that which cannot be said and on which it is impossible to remain silent."

Even normal verbal communication involves tonality. The words we speak are only half the act of communication. Intonation is the other half. The intonations in our voice can change the meaning of words and amplify the force of an act of communication. Music is simply an extension of this aspect of human expression. Singing has always been the most natural thing for people to do.

The psalms also encourage us to use musical instruments to stretch the potential for expression as far as it can go. A skilled musician can use an instrument to express something words cannot reach. The expressive power of music is attested to by the way it seems to have such immediate and direct access to our emotions. In a corporate context, moreover, music can draw people together in a unified expression. The use of music and song is a wonderful way for a congregation of people to declare something in one accord. Music also holds our attention and enables us to reflect on something in a way that nothing else can.

The psalms also encourage the use of physical gestures to express joy. Again, this is a natural extension of a basic element of human communication. We all tend to use physical gestures when we communicate; it is part of our self-expression. As with tonality, we are rarely conscious of the gestures we make in our communication, but they are nevertheless a constant part of it. The psalms exhort us to clap, to lift up our hands, to bow, to kneel, and to dance. Even the most reserved person will relate to the need for physical expression in the most important parts of life. No parent can ever be content with expressing love to his or her children in words alone. Our joy over our children must express itself physically, and so we hug them and kiss them. The only relationship more fundamental to our lives than those of our immediate kin is, of course, our relationship with God, and so it is natural that we should express the joy of this love through physical gestures.

The more we allow ourselves to express our joy in these ways, the more we allow that joy to flow and increase within us. The expression of joy is the basic element of the process of enjoyment itself. To rejoice in God, we must be willing to express ourselves freely. Many people feel embarrassed about expressing themselves in public, particularly in ways they deem to be less than completely dignified. This is one thing we must be prepared to sacrifice if we are to give joy its full expression, just as David was prepared to put dignity aside when he danced before God. In the same way that I am prepared to stoop down and hug my child in public, I must be prepared to be uninhibited in the public expression of my love for God. It is not that we *have* to make certain physical gestures; the point is that we must not allow anything to inhibit us from doing these things. There is nothing more important than loving God, and love naturally expresses itself physically.

When the psalmists exhort us to use physical gestures to praise God, they are not just encouraging uninhibited expression. They are also encouraging us to let other people know that we love God. Such gestures are not pious exhibitionism. They are a public demonstration. They are a physical declaration of unashamed association with God. Praise is all about *letting others know*. This is not showing off; it is simply part of conveying a message about the delightfulness of God. It is the same way we convey our support for a sports team or our appreciation for a great performer. To praise God is not only to say things but also to allow ourselves to use whatever physical expression comes naturally and conveys most effectively our love for him.

The Burden of Praise

Praise is about letting other people know. It is clear from the praise psalms that the heart of praise cannot be satisfied until everyone shares the joy of God. When I say everyone, I mean *everyone on earth*. At its highest expression, praise in the psalms becomes the longing for all peoples of all nations to enjoy and glorify God. It is a repeated motif throughout the psalms of praise and thanksgiving. The vision of a world united in praise to God is the great vision for which the psalms ultimately reach. This is the synergy of communal enjoyment in its highest form, and it is the goal of human history.

> Praise the LORD, all you nations;
> extol him, all you peoples.
> For great is his love toward us,
> and the faithfulness of the LORD endures forever.
>
> Praise the LORD. (Ps. 117)

The compulsion to praise God is therefore the underlying motive that compels us to join with God's mission in the world. Lamentation expresses and amplifies empathy and compassion, but only the experience of the joy of God creates a possibility to reach for in mission. We cannot give what we do not have. If we have the joy of God, though, we will not be able to suppress the desire to impart that joy to others. In the process, we will be led back to where we started in our journey through the spirituality of the psalms, for in a world that lacks the joy of God, the expression of joy is inevitably arrested by the suffering of humanity.

Joy seeks joy. Until everyone shares the same joy, the joyful heart will carry a burden of desire that will lead it back to the sadness of God. The greater our joy, the greater our sadness for those who lack such joy. It is an inevitable cycle that will continue as long as this world remains broken. Only in a new heavens and a new earth can joy be unleashed from this burden. Until then, our joy compels us to share what

173

we have with those who don't have it. The burden of praise is that all people must know. The heart of praise reaches forward to that time envisaged by Isaiah, a time when "the earth will be full of the knowledge of the LORD as the waters cover the sea" (11:9).

CONCLUSION

The Fear of the Lord

I am aware that much of what I have discussed in this book is complex, but let's learn to value complexity. Simplistic, pragmatic approaches to the spiritual life tend not to work in the long run for anyone. They may make us feel good for a while in the light of our achievements and virtues, but ultimately they leave us feeling dead. What truly invigorates the soul is *relationship*. It is what we were made for, and it is what activates our joy. True happiness, that is, the state of being from which joy flows, is a real relationship with the real God.

As soon as we enter the area of relationship, we enter an area of immeasurable complexity. It is complex because we are complex in our dysfunctions, but it is also complex because the experience of personal connectedness with God is so deep and unfathomable. This is what makes it so rich and preserves its freshness. It never runs out of potential for impact. We can't weary of love; we will never have our fill of it, and yet consider how unfathomable a thing love is. There is no understanding relationship from the outside.

An objective understanding is ignorance. To understand a relationship of love, we have to plunge into it with abandon. We have to become a lover.

My advice for you is to spend less time trying to grasp God intellectually and more time allowing yourself to be grasped by God. The psalms were written by people who found out that they could not grasp God. Many psalms portray the struggle it took for them, in many cases, to relinquish objective understanding in order to rest in trust. Once they gave up trying to grasp God, they were in a position to be grasped by God. From this experience came a deeper relational understanding that gave them rest and joy, often in spite of their circumstances.

The governing idea of the biblical wisdom literature, of which the psalms are a part, is expressed in this oft-repeated statement: "The fear of the LORD is the beginning of wisdom" (Ps. 111:10; Prov. 9:10). The book of Job is an extended example of a struggle played out in many psalms. Job tried to fathom how his suffering could fit into God's plan, and in the end he never found out. He never understood God. But he did have a profound encounter with God and a real relationship with God. What Job attained by the end of his ordeal was "the fear of the Lord."

The fear of the Lord is the experience of the breakdown of all our intellectual capacities in the light of the magnitude and glory of God. It is an extreme version of *awe*. To know God's glory and greatness, we have to allow ourselves to be transcended, and this is a frightening experience. It is frightening because it threatens the whole structure of autonomous security within which we are comfortable.

It seems that anyone who encountered the glory of God at any point in the biblical narratives found the experience completely overwhelming. It wasn't a negative experience;

on the contrary, it was intensely positive. It evoked great joy but with great trembling. It was not just a moving experience; it was completely displacing. To use the metaphor from chapter 3, it had the effect of cracking open people's shells and dismantling their autonomous worlds, allowing reality to flood in. But the reality that flooded in was the presence of a loving God, and it was with his love that they were flooded. So it is that after the struggle the psalmists rest peacefully, engulfed in and upheld by the presence of God.

Possibilities

The experience I have observed in the psalms is possible for you. It is not the property of spiritual gurus. It is held out in the psalms to ordinary people like you and me. The psalms themselves tell us, in fact, that it is the *lowly* whom God wants to lift up to this place (25:9; 113:7; 138:6; 145:14). It is those who don't think they qualify that God most wants to reach out to and grasp. The moment we look at the intimacy with God that was attained by the psalmists and say to ourselves, "I can't get there," we are ready for God to work in our lives. It is always God who gets us there. We only have to be willing. If there is an obstacle, then it is in our will.

Most of us intuitively resist moving toward God because of what it will do to our protective shell. We fear the dismantlement of all those dreams and ambitions that had to do with giving ourselves a sense of control over our identity and destiny. So we remain in our shell, and we become believers in a God who is *out there* but not *in here*. Our faith becomes a detached intellectual faith, and our spirituality becomes simple and pragmatic enough to make us feel like everything is all right. The problem is that we end up not feeling much at all.

It is difficult to feel passionate about ideas. It can be done, but we have to constantly look for opportunities to debate and affirm our theology so as to feel "zealous" about it. I went this way for a time in my younger years and ended up as a crusader for orthodoxy with a gaping absence of any real ongoing experience of God. I haven't changed my core beliefs since then, but I have changed how I apply my beliefs. The psalms were a key tool of divine revelation in this transformation.

A Personal Journey

The first thing the psalms did for me was to raise my expectations of what was possible. I had accommodated my expectations to my limited experience. It was not that I had no experience; I just didn't think there was much more available to me than what I was experiencing. As I worked with the psalms, however, I could not deny that the people who wrote them were experiencing a relationship with God that was as real as with any other person. I could also see the effect that this had on their lives. They were expressing peace, joy, and confidence in the face of unimaginable danger. They were enjoying God in praise and worship to a degree that clearly indicated it was more than just pious respect.

The more I read and sang the psalms, the less content I became with where I was. I began to feel empty and alienated, and I recognized from the lament psalms that this is actually a good thing. It was the beginning of my awakening. I could no longer be content without a real experience of relationship with God. So I echoed the complaints of the lament psalms, and I cried out to God. The psalms gave me permission to be discontented with little when so much more had been promised to me. They gave me permission to argue my case before God, and as I did so, I could feel God's pleasure over me as I exercised my faith.

I would love to tell you that God came through straight-away, but he didn't. He left me to seek and wait for a long time. At first this perturbed me, but I saw, again from the psalms, that this was a common experience for God's people. I also began to realize that the process of seeking God was actually changing me profoundly. It was growing my faith and orienting my heart, and as a result, I was much more clearheaded, focused, and peaceful. My desires were being simplified. The more I sought after God, the more I felt that God was all I really needed, and this was intensely liberating. My seeking was also enabling me to begin to receive God *as God*. I started to experience the restfulness of surrendering to God, and the more I surrendered to God, the more he began to dawn in my heart. As this happened, I started to understand those expressions of absolute contentment and simplicity of desire in two of my favorite psalms:

> One thing I ask of the LORD,
>   this is what I seek:
> that I may dwell in the house of the LORD
>   all the days of my life,
> to gaze upon the beauty of the LORD
>   and to seek him in his temple. (Ps. 27:4)

> Yet I am always with you;
>   you hold me by my right hand.
> You guide me with your counsel,
>   and afterward you will take me into glory.
> Whom have I in heaven but you?
>   And earth has nothing I desire besides you.
> My flesh and my heart may fail,
>   but God is the strength of my heart
>   and my portion forever. (Ps. 73:23–26)

The hardest part of the process was the inevitable truths I had to face about myself. Each step closer to God brought me closer to realizing that I was not nearly as virtuous as I had thought. I mean, I knew I was a sinner, but I was happier to accept that in a general and abstract way. All of a sudden, things were coming to light that devastated me. I realized that in so many areas of life *I* was the bad guy, *I* was the selfish and greedy one, *I* was the cause of the problems, and so on. I had become so proficient at defending and justifying myself that these revelations came as a gigantic shock. What was interesting about the experience, however, was that whenever God's light dawned on these things, I never felt the slightest bit condemned. What I sensed was a deep feeling of connection with God as though a great wall had come down. I had encountered the sadness of God over my life, and the moment my heart came into agreement with his sadness, a deep and unshakable joy in the embrace of God began to dawn.

This experience has happened regularly along the path of my life. Every time I feel stagnant and empty, I now assume that there is something in me that is stopping the light from getting through. I assume that I am hiding something from God in my heart. In these times, my heart is like a patch of grass that some object is covering and blocking from the sun so that it gradually goes brown and dies. When you have felt the life of God in you, the feeling of that life draining out becomes very distinct.

Sometimes it takes a long time for the problems to emerge because my recalcitrant heart won't let these things out without a fight. Thankfully, God always provides the vanquishing blow. He always does something that effectively yanks the issue out into the open, and, as painful as those moments are, they are the most precious moments of salvation in my memory. I persistently avoid the pain of these experiences, but thankfully God persistently and lovingly inflicts it on me, and his persistence always wins. These moments of brokenness are the sweetest moments of divine encounter I have known. My metaphor of the ocean and the shell is the best way I can explain it. It is as though the ocean of God's presence breaks in on my shell and engulfs me. The experience I most feared then becomes the moment of my liberation. I find myself suspended weightlessly, resting in and engulfed by the loving presence of God.

After recording the Sons of Korah version of Psalm 51, I remember listening to it and being struck by the paradoxical combination of pain and sweetness in the expression. I was reminded of the time when Ezekiel was given the scroll containing all God's grievances against his people. God told Ezekiel to eat the scroll, and when he did, it tasted as sweet as honey (Ezek. 3:3). This is an apt description of an experience that can regularly be the breakthrough moment for us at any given time in our lives. I would have this experience more often if I didn't spend so much time defending myself against it.

I am so thankful that God regularly interrupts me as I go along in life. And when he does, however painful it may be at times, I have learned to recognize what is happening and express my gratitude. The more I recognize my absolute indebtedness to God for getting me to where I am, the more sensitive I become to him. It is as though the joyful acknowledgment of my dependence were softening the shell of my autonomous world.

It is so empowering to feel that you are part of something so much bigger than yourself. You feel like anything is possible because nothing depends on you. Everything is being orchestrated by God, even your own life. God is doing things, and all we need to do is step into that flow. We don't make life happen. Life happens when we step into the flow of what God is already doing.

One of the most important habits I have adopted in my life is the one most often enjoined to us in the psalms. It is spending regular times praising and thanking God for how he has prevailed in my life. I have found that this sensitizes my heart to what God is doing now. It opens me up to God. As I express my praise and gratitude, it is as though I were opening the door of my heart. When I open the door of my heart to let an expression of praise out, I am also opening the way for God to come in.

One Step at a Time

When we sense what we lack, our immediate reaction is to feel that we need to get things right straightaway. The good news is that there is grace to go slowly. There is no rush because our spiritual status does not depend on how spiritually advanced we are. We only need to be committed to God through Jesus Christ and walk at *his* pace in *his* direction. God's pace is slow, not because he is slow but because he patiently walks with us. It takes time to learn how to live God's way, and God is the most patient teacher in the world.

No doubt you have a sense of the kind of person you want to be. If you respond to that sense by beating yourself up for what you aren't, then you won't get anywhere. You will only end up bruised and immobilized. God accepts you just the way you are. You don't have to become a perfect person to be accepted by God. Until you accept that basic truth, you will not be able to walk forward. So understand that you don't have to work out the entire continuum of the spiritual life all at once. Just focus on the next step. Ask yourself, "What is

God saying to me now?" The future belongs to God; he has the way worked out. If you worry about the route, you will stumble. Just focus on taking the next step. You probably already know what it is. That step is the beginning of your journey. Bon voyage.

Matthew Jacoby is the teaching pastor at Barrabool Hills Baptist Church in Geelong, Australia, and the leading member of the Psalms project band, Sons of Korah. Matthew has a doctorate in philosophical theology from the University of Melbourne. He and his wife Kate have three children.